UNFORGETTABLE WOMEN OF THE CENTURY

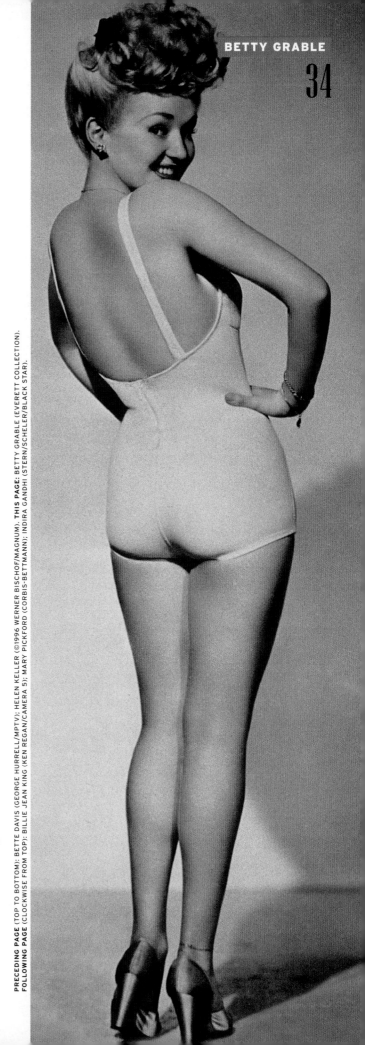

34

STAFF FOR THIS BOOK

EDITOR: Eric Levin
SENIOR EDITOR: Richard Burgheim
ART DIRECTOR: Anthony Wing Kosner
PICTURE EDITOR: Lila Garnett
CHIEF OF REPORTERS: Denise Lynch
SENIOR WRITERS: Allison Adato, Nikki Amdur
CONTRIBUTING WRITERS: Denise Demong,
Marlene McCampbell, J.D. Reed, Lisa Russell,
Cynthia Sanz
REPORTER: Peggy Brawley
DESIGNER: Scott Weiss
RESEARCHER: Steven Cook
COPY EDITOR: Dennison E. Demac
OPERATIONS: Thomas K. Allen

Special thanks to Mim Adkins, Alan Anuskiewicz, Jane Bealer,
Robert Britton, Cara Davis, Kevin Elbert, David Geithner, George Hill,
Suzy Im, Patricia R. Kornberg, Peter Levinson, Rachel Littman,
Eric Mischel, James Oberman, John Silva, Céline Wojtala,
Anna Yelenskaya, the staff of Applied Graphics Technology
and the PEOPLE Edit Tech staff.

Copyright ©1998 Time Inc. Home Entertainment
Published by

A division of Time Inc. Home Entertainment
1271 Avenue of the Americas
New York, NY 10020

PRESIDENT: David Gitow
DIRECTOR, CONTINUITIES AND SINGLE SALES: David Arfine
DIRECTOR, CONTINUITIES AND RETENTION: Michael Barrett
DIRECTOR, NEW PRODUCTS: Alicia Longobardo
GROUP PRODUCT MANAGERS: Robert Fox, Michael Holahan
PRODUCT MANAGERS: Christopher Berzolla, Roberta Harris,
Stacy Hirschberg, Jennifer McLyman, Daniel Melore
MANAGER, RETAIL AND NEW MARKETS: Thomas Mifsud
ASSOCIATE PRODUCT MANAGER: Louisa Bartle, Alison Ehrmann,
Carlos Jimenez, Daria Raehse, Betty Su
ASSISTANT PRODUCT MANAGERS: Meredith Shelley,
Lauren Zaslansky
EDITORIAL OPERATIONS DIRECTOR: John Calvano
FULFILLMENT DIRECTOR: Michelle Gudema
ASSISTANT FULFILLMENT MANAGER: Richard Perez
FINANCIAL DIRECTOR: Tricia Griffin
ASSOCIATE FINANCIAL MANAGER: Amy Maselli
ASSISTANT FINANCIAL MANAGER: Steven Sandonato
MARKETING ASSISTANT: Sarah Holmes

CONSUMER MARKETING DIVISION
BOOK PRODUCTION MANAGER: Jessica McGrath
BOOK PRODUCTION COORDINATOR: Joseph Napolitano

PEOPLE WEEKLY is a registered trademark of Time Inc.
ISBN: 1-883013-36-4
Library of Congress Catalog Card Number: 98-85392

Manufactured in the United States of America

All rights reserved. No part of this book may be reproduced in any form or by any means
without the prior written permission of the publisher, excepting brief quotations in
connection with reviews written specifically for inclusion in magazines and newspapers.

PREVIOUS PAGE: Bette Davis, c. 1939; Helen Keller, 1949.

TABLE OF CONTENTS: Betty Grable, in her famous, morale-
boosting 1942 pinup, proves an exception to the rule "Don't
Look Back"; George Foreman hefts Billie Jean King's trophy
as she displays the $100,000 booty from her 1973 drubbing
of Bobby Riggs; Mary Pickford exhorts a Manhattan crowd
to buy WW I "Liberty Loans"; India's Prime Minister Indira
Gandhi works on matters of state in 1966.

PRECEDING PAGE (TOP TO BOTTOM): BETTE DAVIS (GEORGE HURRELL/MPTV); HELEN KELLER (©1996 WERNER BISCHOF/MAGNUM). THIS PAGE: BETTY GRABLE (EVERETT COLLECTION). FOLLOWING PAGE (CLOCKWISE FROM TOP): BILLIE JEAN KING (KEN REGAN/CAMERA 5); MARY PICKFORD (CORBIS-BETTMANN); INDIRA GANDHI (STERN/SCHELER/BLACK STAR).

Contents

ICONS

Jackie

*She was America's pillar of
strength and paragon of style*

JACQUELINE BOUVIER GREW UP WITH PRIVATE STABLES
and boarding schools, reading Chekhov at age 6. She was
apolitical but married into a roguish, roughhouse political
family that played touch football as she sat on the sidelines.
She was a First Lady of pillbox hats and cello concerts. She was
a widow, tragically, of youth. She weathered a difficult second
marriage, then became unofficial First Lady of the World. We

"I have never met anyone like her," said JFK (with Jackie in Virginia, months before his death) after an early date with his future wife.

An athlete from youth, Jackie took the children skiing in Switzerland.

fondly remember all these lives.

But Jacqueline Bouvier Kennedy Onassis likely would have dismissed such descriptions; she preferred to think of herself just as the mother of John Jr. and Caroline, whom she was determined to raise privately. Her own public life began at 18, when Jackie was singled out as Queen Deb of the Year. She met Senator John Kennedy in 1950 at a dinner party. They married three years later—a smart move on Kennedy's part.

Her polish gave his presidency its glamor. She replaced White House reproductions with authentic period pieces and opened its doors to 80 million people on a televised tour. She moved fashion forward by throwing off the dowdy, pinched dresses of the Eisenhower era for streamlined gowns and suits by Givenchy and Balenciaga. And when JFK's 1,037 days in the White House ended, she taught people to mourn, planning every detail of a funeral modeled after Lincoln's, and quoting her husband's favorite musical to a reporter, insuring that those years would be immortalized as "Camelot." So inspiring was she as a widow, the picture of strength and dignity, that the public resented it when she wed Greek shipping tycoon Aristotle Onassis in 1968.

Again she was widowed, and again we accepted her back into the fold of cherished celebrity. She returned to New York City, where she raised her children, worked as a book editor and battled to save landmark buildings. Quietly, she became a grandmother. Without notice, she enjoyed a long romance with financier Maurice Tempelsman. And, equally privately, she battled lymphoma. When she died at age 64, in 1994, she was buried next to her husband, their stillborn daughter and the son who had lived only three days. "She makes you feel you could do almost anything," said a friend. "Any man married to Jackie probably would have to become President of the United States." ∎

JACKIE WEDS BLANK CHECK headlined a tabloid of her 1968 marriage to Onassis.

"She cared most about being a good mother," said President Clinton in his eulogy.

Princess Diana

HER 16-YEAR REIGN AS PRINCESS OF Wales was more of a blessing for her world of admirers and, however grudgingly, for the House of Windsor than for Diana Spencer herself. Born with a natural if girlish noblesse, she met Charles back when she was 16. But Diana was still a shy kindergarten aide when the

"At the age of 19, you think you're prepared for everything," Diana said later.

prince proposed marriage to her at a place that foreshadowed the tragedy ahead—just outside the garden of his mistress Camilla Parker Bowles's estate.

Diana transformed herself quickly and gracefully from a very private girl-about-London to the planet's most public personage. But as she grew wise to the time-encrusted ways of the Palace, the naïve romantic came to understand that she had been anointed because of her background and lack of any (she had to be a virgin) and her palpable promise as a consort and breeder. "I had tremendous hopes in my heart," she said of the marriage, and they were crushed almost immediately when she discovered that Charles's heart still belonged to Camilla.

The once joyous Diana became so frightfully unhappy that she staged dramatic if ineffective attempts at suicide, like throwing herself down the stairs. Soon the beleaguered princess was to become a tabloid queen as his-and-her affairs, down to embarrassing phone-tapped conversations and tacky nicknames, spilled into the international press. The couple divorced, and Diana's ex-mother-in-law imposed yet another change: Diana would no longer be addressed as Her Royal Highness.

But the people had already crowned Diana as their princess, and forever. She not only had borne and splendidly nurtured two heirs but also had fulfilled missions of her own. She had reached out to AIDS patients, championed land-mine reform and helped destigmatize eating disorders, which she herself had suffered. She had become a style-setting beauty of unmatched charisma, at last comfortable in her own skin. As a single mum of 36, she was ready again—except for the oppressive flashbulbs—for love, and met a man who made her happy. Then, on a fateful summer night in Paris, in 1997, she and Dodi Fayed were killed in a car accident. The first truly 20th century princess had become a heart-breaking legend. ■

A 1993 outing is a poignant memory for Harry and Wills.

A Washington, D.C., girl at a home for children with AIDS met, and moved, Diana in 1990.

Katharine *H*epburn

Forthright and fearless, she wore the pants in Hollywood

S A CHILD, KATHARINE HEPBURN RECALLED, SHE would race down the beach outside her family's Connecticut home, "shouting to myself as I ran about how I was going to save the world." She added, "I think young girls have this powerful sense that, somehow, they're going to change the world."

Hepburn can look back now over her 90 years and feel pleased that she actually did. In an acting career that comprised 44 films and won her an unequaled four Oscars (for *Morning Glory, Guess Who's Coming to Dinner, The Lion in Winter, On Golden Pond*), the confident star with the crisp, aristocratic New England accent and penchant for wearing trousers helped formulate on film the image of the modern woman. "It can be said frankly that Hepburn has not grown up to Hollywood," director George Cukor once said. "Hollywood has grown up to her."

She broke conventions offscreen as well. After a failed six-year marriage in her 20s to a socialite insurance broker, Hepburn said, she "lived like a man," dating such well-known names as Howard Hughes and the married director John Ford but never again striding down the aisle. Then came her romance with actor Spencer Tracy, a Roman Catholic too guilt-plagued to get a divorce during his 27 years with Hepburn. To her it didn't matter what others thought, or even that the alcoholic Tracy (who died in 1967) could be abusive to her. In love, and in life (they costarred in nine films), she has had no regrets. "I've just done what I damn well wanted to," she once told Barbara Walters. "I've made enough money to support myself, and I ain't afraid of being alone." ■

Kate the Great (in 1940, far left, and on location for *The Lion in Winter* in 1968) once said of her appeal, "I think it's because I chose a road and stuck to it."

Amelia Earhart

A jaunty adventurer in a flying machine lifted Depression despair

AMELIA EARHART BRISTLED IN PRIVATE AT being called Lady Lindy. She hated being compared to a man—even one so accomplished as Charles Lindbergh. But long before she vanished above the South Pacific, Earhart had earned her sobriquet. She racked up a string of female firsts—the first to solo across the Atlantic in 1932, to break the cross-continental speed record and to co-own an airline (Transcontinental, with Eugene Vidal). Each new landmark, gained with fearless aplomb, cemented her celebrity. Her cropped hair, smart slacks and leather flying jacket were fascinating in the man's world of the Great Depression. She was, said Gore Vidal, novelist son of Earhart's partner, "beyond stardom. It was a strange continuum that she and Lindbergh occupied. They were like gods from outer space. People would just stand and stare at her." And listen, too. "We must earn true respect and equal rights from men," she told adoring Purdue coeds in 1935, "by accepting responsibility."

Earhart was less confident, though, about matters of the heart and found herself leaning on a man, publisher George Putnam, her unflagging promoter and the financier of her record attempts. He was divorced and begged her to marry him. She acquiesced in 1931 but only after demanding that she be allowed to get out after a year if the marriage didn't work. Apparently it did, for Putnam helped plan and pay for what was to be her crowning achievement: circumnavigating the globe. When she and navigator Fred Noonan took off from Miami, they had parachutes, but they later left them behind to save weight. It was a mistake. On July 2, 1937, some 22,000 miles into her 27,000-mile trek, Earhart lifted off from New Guinea for the 2,550-mile leg to tiny Howland Island. She and Noonan never made it. Just three weeks before her 40th birthday, Amelia Earhart disappeared into thin air.

Over the years there were many theories about what had happened, with no conclusive proof. Among them was speculation that Earhart had been shot down while taking pictures of Japanese bases for the U.S. military. But it is the Earhart mystery and romance we cling to. "Because she died young," says Nancy Porter, who produced a PBS documentary on the flier, "your final image of her is frozen in time." And in the heart. Had she gone down in today's tabloid age, there would no doubt be Amelia sightings. ∎

The aviatrix displays the élan (circa 1936) that captivated America. The plane, a twin-engine Lockheed Electra, is the type of craft in which she perished.

Mother Teresa

She found God's spirit and her calling, aiding society's outcasts

"Sometimes a good feeling inside is worth much more than a beautician," Teresa (here blessing a nun) once advised.

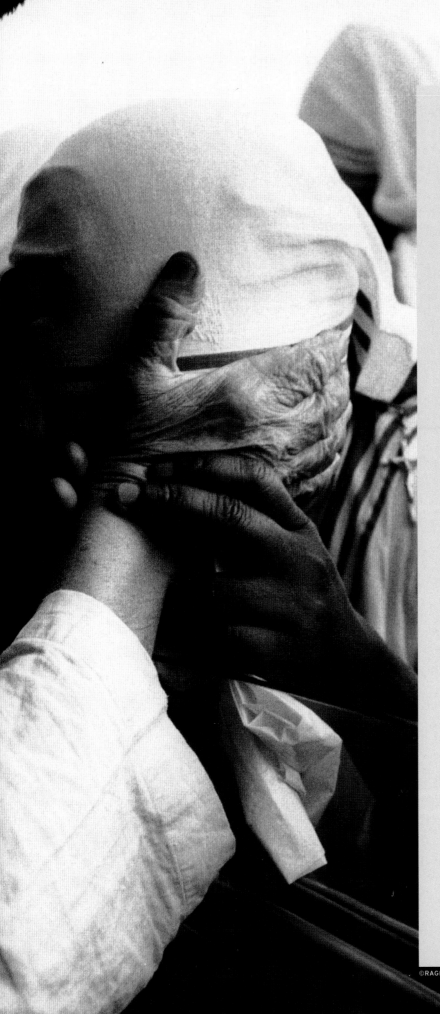

IN AN INSTANT OF DIVINE INSPIRA-
tion, she saw her future, but it took
her two years to convince the Vati-
can to trust the boldness of her
vision. While riding on a train in India,
Sister Teresa decided that she must
leave her cloister in Calcutta, where she
taught upper-class Bengali girls, and
devote herself to helping the wretched
of the streets. She had come far in every
sense from the Albanian village where
she grew up as Agnes Gonxha Bojaxhiu,
daughter of a building contractor who
died when she was 7. Now, at 36, after 18
years in quiet service as a nun, she
would begin an even greater journey.
Finally winning Rome's approval,
Mother Teresa stunningly challenged
the caste system of her adopted country
by opening a treatment center for the
most reviled of India's untouchables: the
lepers. With the establishment of the
Missionaries of Charity in 1950, the
barefoot nun in the blue-and-white
habit became a familiar sight in Calcutta's teeming slums.

Singleminded in her mission, she
was unfazed by criticism of her accepting donations from scoundrels like S&L
czar Charles Keating and associating
with Haitian strongman "Baby Doc"
Duvalier. Despite their sins, the cash
enabled her to establish outposts in
more than 120 countries. One of the
troubled souls she befriended in her
travels was Princess Diana (the two
once shared a tête-à-tête at her South
Bronx center). But even Diana had to
wait in line to see the woman affection-
ately nicknamed "the saint of the gut-
ters." Mother Teresa was unimpressed
by wealth and position, observing, "I
find the rich much poorer—sometimes
they are more lonely inside"; and she
once said that a beggar's contribution of
a coin was worth more to her than her
1979 Nobel Peace Prize. That no doubt
was why thousands of the poor braved
monsoon rains to honor their beloved
Angel of Calcutta when, at 87, the tiny
nun's big heart finally failed her. ∎

Oprah *Winfrey*

The queen of dish won't talk trash but remains first in the hearts of her countrywomen

This 1994 Emmy is just one of her show's 25. At 44, Oprah has mentees but no kids of her own, figuring, "I can make a greater contribution to the world's children."

"OPRAH," WRITER FRAN LEBOWITZ once summed up, "is probably the greatest media influence on the adult population. She is almost a religion." Or at least the mammon of the media. From her talk show base, she moves mountains of books, produces TV programming and films and was herself nominated for a supporting-actress Oscar in 1985 for *The Color Purple*. *Forbes* has reckoned her net worth at $550 million, making Winfrey the world's wealthiest woman entertainer.

That she was born female, black, poor and illegitimate in rural Mississippi in 1954 makes her rise even more remarkable. She credits her father, a Nashville barber who took custody of her after she ran away at 13. While on scholarship at Tennessee State University, she was hired as a local news anchor. Then in 1984, she turned around a faltering Chicago talk show by dumping food and beauty features in favor of hot-button topics like divorce. Buoyed by her humor, empathy and willingness to share her heroic personal struggles with obesity and childhood sexual abuse, it was syndicated and soared to No. 1 in national ratings—until she publicly swore off tawdry topics, declaring, "I won't have people yelling and screaming and trying to humiliate one another." With her fiancé of six years, marketing exec Stedman Graham, she uses her clout to help inner city families. Oprah's mission, she says, is for "people to have the grandest vision for their lives." ∎

Martha Graham

She made ballet dance to her stark, impassioned tune

AS SURELY AS PICASSO CHANGED ART, CHOREographer Martha Graham transformed dance. To a world accustomed to classic ballet's soaring leaps and toes *en pointe*, she introduced a movement style that was stage-bound and angular and, frequently, violent and erotic. It was in the 1930s that she formed her own company, because, as she put it, "I did not dance the way that people danced." Her goal was to convey emotion. "I don't want to be understandable," she declared. "I want to be felt." Over 70 years, Graham worked with great names in music (Copland, Stravinsky), ballet (Balanchine, Baryshnikov) and even acting (Bette Davis and Joanne Woodward were among her students).

Her love life was bound up in her art, beginning with composer Louis Horst, who would be her romantic and creative partner for two decades. Next came the thrilling young dancer Erick Hawkins, for whom she choreographed the beloved "Appalachian Spring." When she was 54, Graham wed Hawkins, 39, and, in the words of Agnes de Mille, "walked straight into the trap that greatly gifted women are apt to walk into when they fall in love: The man can't stand the inferior position." Hawkins couldn't. "He divided our money, left a note and was gone," wrote Graham. "I was shattered." Still, her despair seemed far greater when she reluctantly retired at 75 and began drinking herself, friends feared, to her death. Three years later, Graham decided that "I would bloom again," and she resumed choreographing and directing, staging 20 new dances and more than 30 major revivals before cardiac arrest finally claimed her, in 1991, at age 96. ∎

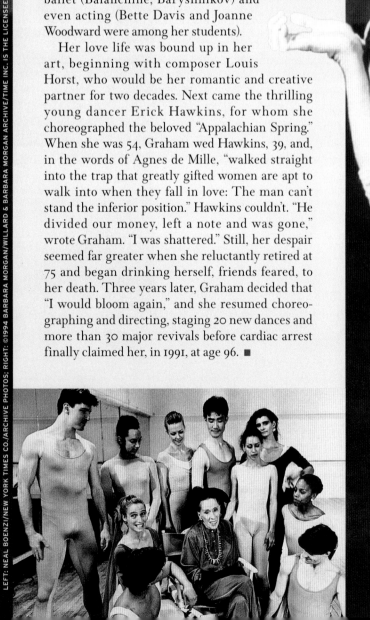

In 1940, at age 46, Graham choreographed a tribute to Emily Dickinson—and four decades later was still running her company of dancer disciples in Manhattan (left).

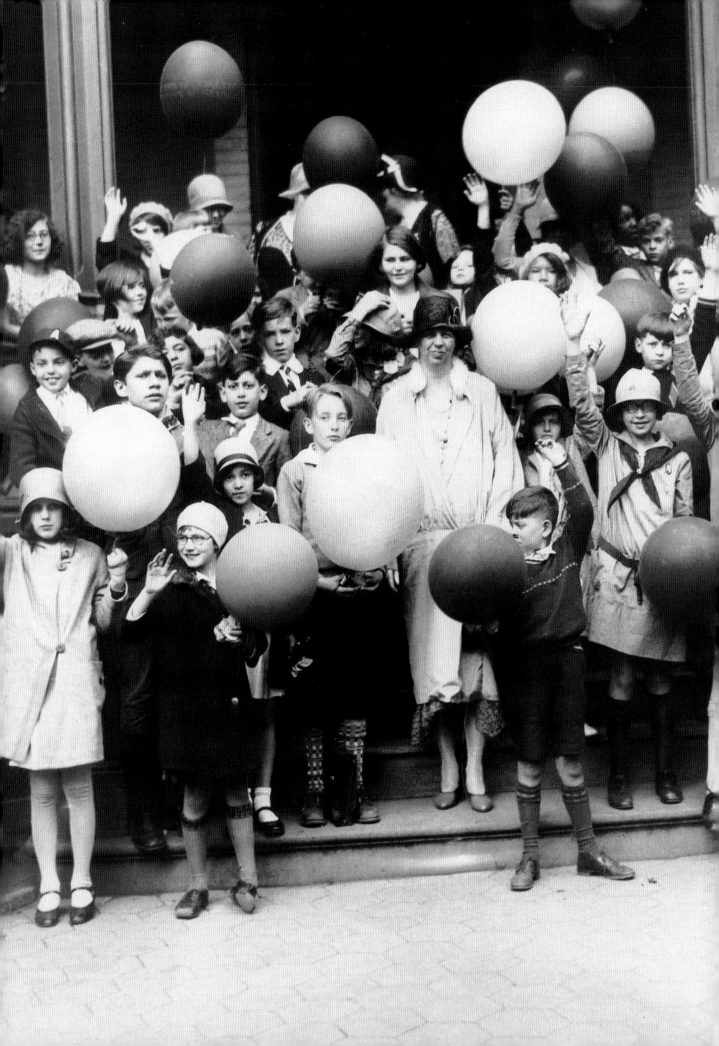

Eleanor *R*oosevelt

FDR's envoy at large was a world champion of human rights

A T 64, ELEANOR ROOSEVELT HAS become perhaps the best-known woman in the world," pronounced TIME in 1948. So she was, and so much more. Through her impassioned advocacy of the rights of women, children and the downtrodden, she became America's social conscience. But she downplayed her deeds, explaining, "I just did what I had to do as things came along."

What came along was history—and hurt. The shy, 20-year-old Eleanor wed her fifth cousin Franklin Delano Roosevelt in 1905 and bore six children, one of whom died in infancy. But it was in 1918, she later wrote, that "the bottom dropped out of my particular world": She discovered that her husband was carrying on an affair with her social secretary Lucy Mercer. Through months of soul-searching, Eleanor fought her shock and anger. But in the end, her marriage endured to become a union of mutual respect and world-changing shared leadership.

Rumors flew about her own romantic life, including an affair with a bodyguard, and, although nothing was ever substantiated, possible lesbian relationships. Her journalist friend Lorena Hickok wrote Eleanor, "I remember your eyes, with a kind of teasing smile in them, and the feeling of that soft spot just north-east of the corner of your mouth against my lips."

Whatever private turmoil she suffered, the public Eleanor blossomed, playing a major role in the 12-year presidency of her wheelchair-bound husband. She traveled the world as his fact finder and ambassador, and crusaded to bring women into government and to establish daycare centers. After FDR's death in 1945, she continued to lecture and write until her death from tuberculosis in 1962. Without question America's most powerful First Lady, she was also, in the words of historian Arthur Schlesinger Jr., "a great and gallant—and above all, a profoundly good—lady." ∎

A lady for all causes, not the least children, she visited a Brooklyn museum in 1929, above, and brought her moral force to bear as U.S. delegate to the UN two decades later.

Anne Frank

She gave lyrical words and a face to the unfathomable

I T SEEMS TO ME THAT LATER ON NEITHER I NOR ANY one else will be interested in the musings of a 13-year-old schoolgirl," Anne Frank wrote in a 1942 diary entry, one of her first. Despite these misgivings she kept at it, urged on by the knowledge that she was living in historic times in Holland. The diary recorded her first kiss, her C- in algebra and the tiffs with her older sister Margot. It could be the minutia of any young girl's life, except, maybe, Anne was a little more bookish than the average teen: She made notes about stories she would someday have her own children read. But occasional passages betray her unusual and harrowing circumstances: "I get frightened . . . when I think of close friends who are now at the mercy of the cruelest monsters ever to stalk the earth. And all because they're Jews."

Hidden from the world for two years after her family and four of their friends had moved into a "secret annex" behind her father's office, Anne turned inward to compose an astoundingly self-aware journal of her life. From the radio poured news of the Allied struggle against the Nazis—the nightmare backdrop for her adolescent frustrations, fears and dreams. The diary ends abruptly (in the midst of a meditation on her reputation as "boy-crazy, as well as a flirt, a smart aleck and a reader of romances") on Aug. 1, 1944, three days before the eight lodgers in the annex were arrested by the Gestapo for the crime of being Jewish in Nazi-occupied Amsterdam. Miep Gies, an employee of Anne's father, discovered the diary hours after the Franks had left. She held on to it, along with the rest of Anne's papers, including a novel she had started to write, hoping to return them to her at war's end. But in 1945, at age 15, Anne died of typhus while imprisoned in Bergen-Belsen. A month later the camp was liberated by British troops. Some have called her diary, which was published in 1947, the voice of the 6 million Jews who were silenced. It is never less than the voice of Anne: Anne the student, Anne the daughter, Anne the witness, telling the world—now, in more than 25 million copies in 58 languages—I was here. ∎

"Paper has more patience than people," Anne wrote in 1942 before going into hiding.

As a girl, Anne (right, circa 1937) played with pals on the sidewalks of Amsterdam.

"Emancipation of women has made them lose their mystery," Kelly (in 1954) once remarked.

Grace Kelly

In Monaco's gilded cage, she played her toughest role, as princess and mother

EVEN BEFORE GRACE KELLY MARRIED A prince, she had the aura of a princess. But beneath the exquisite exterior beat the heart of a spunky Irish girl from Philadelphia, who pursued acting with the same determination that had transformed her brash, bricklayer father into a masonry millionaire. As a teenager, Kelly worked as a model and, rich man's daughter though she was, plowed her earnings into paying her way through drama school. In Hollywood, director Alfred Hitchcock once recalled, "they all said at first she was too cold, sexless. But to me she was always . . . a snow-covered volcano." In such classics as *Rear Window* (with Jimmy Stewart) and *High Society* (Bing Crosby), and in her Oscar-winning title role in *The Country Girl*, in 1954, Kelly proved Hitchcock correct.

She enjoyed a string of ardent, famous lovers, including Clark Gable, Ray Milland, Oleg Cassini and the Shah of Iran. Then, in 1954, Kelly was introduced to Monaco's Prince Rainier at the Cannes Film Festival. Completely smitten, the prince kept her in his sights until he managed to wangle a Christmas invitation to her family's home the next year. Two weeks later the couple were engaged, though Grace admitted, "I barely know him. I don't know what will happen." Monégasques initially viewed their movie-star princess skeptically, much as mainline Philadelphians had snubbed her self-made father. But through her charity work, Grace earned Monaco's respect. "Never forget that Grace was a working woman," friend and bridesmaid Judy Quine pointed out. "She took her experience as an actress and applied it to being a princess, a wife and a mother. She knew life was not simple."

Indeed not. Her oldest, Caroline—an impetuous Kelly to the core—nearly broke Grace's heart by running off with French playboy Philippe Junot, and Stephanie worrisomely tended to prefer nightlife over homelife. Grace missed her shy son Albert, away in the navy. She grew restless within the palace walls and considered resuming her film career—Hitchcock offered her the lead in 1964's *Marnie*—but Rainier disapproved. Grace did not get the chance to resolve the conflict. In 1982, while driving toward home in the South of France with Stephanie beside her, she suffered a stroke. The car plunged off the twisty mountain road. Stephanie, 17, was barely scratched; Grace, 52, never regained consciousness. ∎

After their 1956 wedding, Rainier and his bride honeymooned on the royal yacht.

Returning from France and a rare vacation in 1950, Keller received a message in sign language from the fingers of a companion.

Helen Keller

Her amazingly full life was an achievement that inspired the world

THE ACCOMPLISHMENTS ARE ALL BUT unfathomable: She could not see. She could not hear. Yet Helen Keller mastered five languages, wrote countless articles and 14 books, and had a long career as a lecturer and crusader for social reform.

Born in 1880 in Tuscumbia, Alabama, Keller was 19 months old when a severe fever erased her vision and hearing. Sealed off from the world, she grew into a wild, unruly child until she was 6, when deliverance arrived in the form of 20-year-old Anne Sullivan. After taming her rages, Sullivan broke through—as immortalized in the play and movie *The Miracle Worker*—by spilling water over one of Helen's hands as she spelled "water" into the other. Suddenly, Keller later recounted, "the mystery of language was returned to me."

Within months she learned Braille and typing, and by placing her fingers on a teacher's throat, she discerned the vibrations of speech. At Radcliffe College, Sullivan spelled lectures into her palm and, in 1904, stood on the platform as her protégé graduated cum laude.

Those who met Keller on the speech circuit were usually struck by her ebullience. But her failure to wed was a lasting sorrow. At 36, she fell in love with a 29-year-old newspaperman, and they planned a secret wedding until her mother broke it up. Keller later called this "unexpected" love "a little island of joy surrounded by dark waters." During World War II, she toured military hospitals to lift morale—a mission she called "the crowning experience of my life." Two decades later, in 1968, she suffered a series of strokes and died at 87. ■

Keller (left) "hears" by feeling the lips of teacher Anne Sullivan, Helen's partner for what she called 50 "inseparable" years.

Audrey *Hepburn*

"She's a wispy little thing," said director Billy Wilder of Hepburn (in 1953). "But you're really in the presence of somebody when you see that girl."

The lithe beauty of stylish romantic comedies showed her true grace not through couture but caring

CHIC WITHOUT TRYING," IS HOW ONE AWE-struck designer described the wardrobe that epitomized Audrey: sleeveless black shifts, capri pants and ballet flats. Givenchy created the clothes, but Hepburn, charming her way through films like *Breakfast at Tiffany's* and *Funny Face*, brought the threads to life. She insisted that any woman could attain her look: Just buy the dress. Nice of her to say, but no. Her innate elegance ran deeper. Born in Belgium to a Dutch baroness and a British banker, who were soon divorced, Edda van Heemstra Hepburn-Ruston was raised in Nazi-occupied Holland. Her much-admired, slender frame was in part the result of malnutrition during her teens, when she worked for the Resistance. Given the circumstances, she did not think herself beautiful and once remarked that she wished she had curves like other female stars of the day. Married and divorced twice, Hepburn in 1968

essentially ended a career honored by five Academy Award nominations (and one win, for *Roman Holiday*) to spend more time with her children Sean Ferrer (her son with actor Mel) and Luca Dotti (her son with psychiatrist Andrea). A recipient of international relief in the aftermath of World War II, Hepburn in 1988 became UNICEF's special ambassador, turning the public's fascination with her into attention to the world's underprivileged children. (Though she never forgot the power of a Givenchy garment. "When I talk about UNICEF on television, I am naturally emotional," she told the couturier. "Wearing your blouse makes me feel protected.") When she died in 1993 of colon cancer, at 63, the world lost more than a fine actress. It lost an heroic soul. Compassion came to Audrey Hepburn as effortlessly as style. ∎

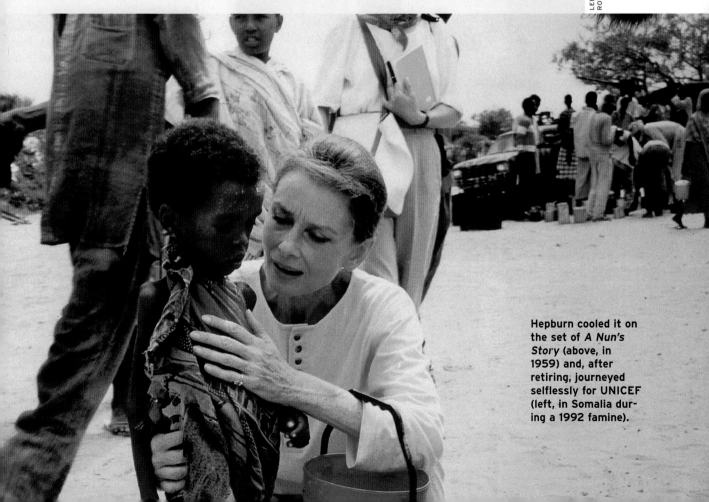

Hepburn cooled it on the set of *A Nun's Story* (above, in 1959) and, after retiring, journeyed selflessly for UNICEF (left, in Somalia during a 1992 famine).

Georgia O'Keeffe

For the painter and muse, beauty was a strong sense of place

SHE MADE HER MARK ON THE WORLD WITH bold, persimmon-colored poppies, sculptural calla lilies and cow skulls as elegant as fine china, all magnified and rendered on large-scale canvases that the prewar art establishment could not ignore. Her dream of becoming an artist dated back to when Georgia Totto O'Keeffe was a 10-year-old farm girl in a large Wisconsin family. Her earliest memory, she once said, was of "the brightness of light—light all around." Her life's work would be to capture that light in paint. By the time she was 28, a show of her early charcoal drawings hung in a prestigious New York City gallery owned by photographer Alfred Stieglitz, who had given Pablo Picasso his first American exhibition. She never signed her work, but O'Keeffe developed a style that was unmistakable. Years later she became the first woman honored with a retrospective at the Museum of Modern Art—one that included many of her famously sensual flower canvases. (Sensual, yes, but not sexual, insisted O'Keeffe, resisting a common description of her oeuvre.)

Her early meeting with Stieglitz, 23 years her senior, led to a partnership that was professional (he was her patron in lean times and mounted 20 O'Keeffe shows) as well as personal (they wed after he divorced his first wife in 1924). Before their marriage, however, the couple caused a buzz when Stieglitz exhibited a show that included 45 nude photographs of O'Keeffe. The pictures were of course his, but with her forthright and unashamed presence in the photos, O'Keeffe put her artistic mark on them. Her love affair with Stieglitz waned in later years and was outlasted by her passion for the Southwest. When he died, in 1946, she moved to New Mexico, living reclusively and working prolifically for three decades. O'Keeffe painted, she said, to "say things with color and shapes that I couldn't say in any other way—things I had no words for." By 1971 failing eyesight had ended her career. She died, in 1986, at age 98, completely blind to the sunlit, natural beauty she had made generations stop and gaze at in wonder. ■

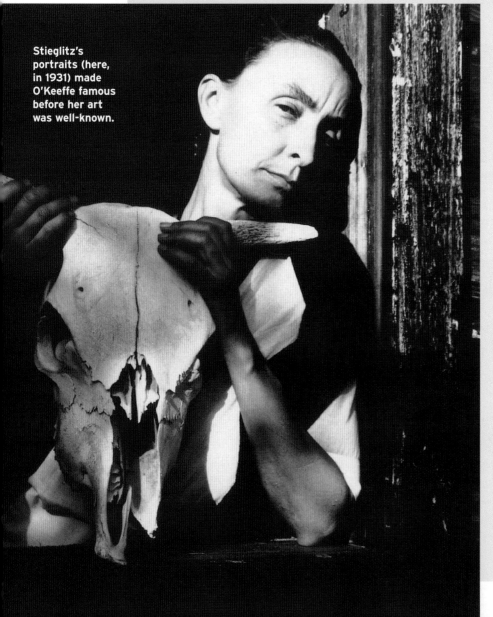

Stieglitz's portraits (here, in 1931) made O'Keeffe famous before her art was well-known.

Aware from an early age of societal limitations on women, O'Keeffe (at home, age 90) concluded, "At least I could paint as I wanted."

All-Am

WINNING WASN'T THE ONLY THING, BUT THEY DID IT WITH RED-WHITE-AND-TRUE GRIT EVEN IF SINGING THE BLUES

Doris Day

A string of bubbly roles made her the model of pert pulchritude, but her reality was no pajama game

erican

ALTHOUGH THE CAREER OF THE former Doris von Kappelhoff of Cincinnati (she plucked her *nom de film* from a song, "Day by Day") spanned three decades, it never allowed her to grow up, freezing Doris Day into perpetual All-American-Girl status. She was the girl in Bob Crosby's band, the girl next door and the labor-union loyalist (in 1957's *The Pajama Game*). She was later the virgin in sex farces with Rock Hudson (one of which, *Pillow Talk*, earned her an Oscar nomination). Actor Oscar Levant joked, "I knew Doris Day before she was a virgin."

She retired from film at 44, in 1968, when *With Six You Get Eggroll* was released during the throes of the sexual revolution. Although she had challenged audi-

ence expectation in Hitchcock's *The Man Who Knew Too Much*, she turned down the chance to be Mrs. Robinson in *The Graduate*. Her sunny onscreen persona contrasted with Day's personal reality, which included four husbands. The third one picked her cookie-cutter roles, then lost the fortune she had earned, forcing her to return to work on a TV series he'd committed her to before his death in 1968. (She later sued a former lawyer for $22 million and won.) When she wrote her 1975 autobiography and discussed her virginal image, Day said, "My first husband was not my first lover. . . . I was a singer on the road with a band at 16, so I don't think that should surprise anyone." So she's not Snow White, but, though she hasn't taken a role since '73, Day remains, indelibly, forever our girl. ■

Grable's gams (in 1945) were insured by Lloyds of London for $1 million—more than Fred Astaire's or Marlene Dietrich's.

Betty Grable

Hers was a career with legs

THE OBJECT OF MANY A GUY'S fantasy, Betty Grable was a realist. "I couldn't outdance Ginger Rogers or Eleanor Powell," she once said. "As a singer I'm no rival to Doris Day. As an actress I don't take myself seriously. Maybe I had sincerity. And warmth." And legs. Her famous 1942 pinup—in a white bathing suit and an over-the-shoulder smile—boosted Allied morale from Salerno to the Solomon Islands. More than 3-million prints were made, and copies were even found in the possession of captured German and Japanese soldiers.

Her movies, though numerous, were not memorable. She had appeared in some 30 films before getting a break on Broadway in *DuBarry Was a Lady*. She then returned to Hollywood as a headliner. The best of her pictures were successful because, as with *How to Marry a Millionaire*, they had costars like Marilyn Monroe or Lauren Bacall. For the most part they were confections, usually something about a college coed with great legs or the backstage life of a showgirl with great legs. By 1943, Grable was the top box-office draw. "My films never once got a good review," she said, but "even the grandmothers wrote me fan letters."

Her personal relationships were less reliable. Married briefly to former child star Jackie Coogan, Grable wed bandleader Harry James in 1943. They had two children but could not find a stable family life. They drank and gambled and lost their fortunes. James had affairs, and in 1965 they divorced. Grable stayed onstage until 1972. When she died of cancer a year later, at 56, the queen of the pinups was eulogized as "she who unofficially won the war." ■

Said FDR to King George VI: "This is Kate Smith. Miss Smith *is* America." During the war, she readied an airmail special delivery.

Kate Smith

God blessed America with her great, patriotic pipes

"I don't practice . . . I save it for when it's necessary," said Smith (on TV in 1965).

S HE DIDN'T SPEAK UNTIL SHE WAS 4, AND THEN SHE MADE UP for it with a voice so robust it helped get a shaky nation through World War II. Smith recorded over 3,000 songs and traveled half-a-million miles to entertain the troops and sell $600 million in war bonds at home. The singer, who never took a lesson ("It would spoil the natural gift," she said), had already wowed WW I vets at 8, inspiring her to head north to Broadway at 17, though her Virginia businessman father wanted her to become a nurse.

Weighing 200 pounds, Smith started out in a comedy act as the butt of Bert Lahr's fat jokes. After the show she would weep in her dressing room. Columbia Records rep Ted Collins rescued her, getting her a radio show on which, in 1938, she introduced her trademark "God Bless America." Nearly 40 years later the song became the good-luck charm for hockey's Philadelphia Flyers, when they won the Stanley Cup in 1974 after she performed it live. Styles changed, but Smith, who said no to marriage five times ("I passed it up for my career and the public"), kept belting out tunes with Yankee-Doodle cheer. She struggled with diabetes for years before she died in 1986, at 77, and always found something positive in the current pop scene. "I like John Denver," she once said. "He's very American." ■

Shirley Temple
From little angel to ambassador

"I CLASS MYSELF WITH RIN TIN TIN," SAYS Shirley Temple Black of her place in Hollywood history. "At the end of the Depression, people were looking for something to cheer themselves up. They fell in love with a dog and a little girl. It won't happen again." Maybe not, but that has to do as much with the little girl as with the times she was born to. When Shirley was a toddler in Santa Monica, her mother took her to dancing school to learn tap, tango and rhumba. There a studio scout plucked her (and 11 others) for small roles in short films called *Baby Burlesks*. But of the lot of tots, only Shirley went on to feature films. Soon she was earning $1,000 a week (her father squandered most of her earnings in poor investments). On her eighth birthday she received gifts from 135,000 well-wishers worldwide. Cute, she was also camera-wise beyond her years. "That Temple kid scares me," remarked costar Adolphe Menjou. "She knows all the tricks. She backs me out of the camera, blankets me, grabs my laughs. She's making a stooge of me. She's an Ethel Barrymore at 4."

Temple generally played a singing moppet whose twinkly eyes and dimples helped redeem a ne'er-do-well. Her precocity impelled one straightlaced Catholic group to investigate whether Shirley was in fact an adult midget sashaying suggestively. But as Shirley grew, her star fell. At 17, she wed a classmate's brother who wanted to be in pictures with her. The marriage ended after a year and one child. She then married Navy man Charlie Black and retired at 22 to be a mom and political volunteer. In 1969 she launched a career in diplomacy, first at the UN under Nixon, later as Ambassador to Ghana and Czechoslovakia. Says Black: "Long ago I became more interested in the real world than in make-believe." ■

"I stopped believing in Santa Claus at an early age," says Black (in '34 and at the '98 Oscars). "Mother took me to see him in a department store, and he asked for my autograph."

"It bothers me that there is an image of me being so ... nauseatingly good," says Field (in 1965).

SallyField
Going public with her insecurities, a gifted actor made Hollywood more real

WHEN SHE DEBUTED AS JULIET AT PASADENA Junior High, her actor mother told her, "Sal, you have magic," and, following her senior year, family friend Eddie Foy invited her to test for the TV version of *Gidget*. A cheerleader and quintessential Valley Girl, she was perfect for the boy-crazy part; and though the series died within a year, Sally Field took wing. Literally, sad to say. At 21, she became the star of *The Flying Nun*. The series was a success—if a national joke—and the perennially insecure Field recalls not realizing that the laugh was on "the Flying Nun and not me." Her struggle with self-esteem became painfully public in 1985 with her "You like me right now! You like me!" comment on national television. The occasion, of course, was her acceptance of the Oscar for *Places in the Heart*. You would think that she'd been under a rock, but it was actually her second

Best Actress award (*Norma Rae* was the first, in 1980).

Field's "crippling shyness," she says, was rooted in her parents' divorce when she was 4. Her mother, Margaret, soon remarried an intimidating actor, Jock Mahoney (a movie Tarzan and TV's Yancy Derringer). After a failed first marriage of her own, Field says she began to gain confidence during a five-year affair with Burt Reynolds, which began with the film *Smokey and the Bandit* in 1977. "Burt was this very vigorous, attractive man," Field said, "and he really helped a lot in just being attracted to me." Blockbuster hits like *Mrs. Doubtfire* and *Forrest Gump* didn't hurt. And now on her own (a second marriage broke up in 1994), with her third son, Sam, born in 1987, Field feels as strong as the Steel Magnolia she played in 1989, saying, "I don't need somebody with me to make me whole." For the first time, Sally Field really, really likes herself. ∎

Field was embarrassed by the Sister Bertrille gig: "You couldn't watch Johnny Carson or Bob Hope without seeing a *Flying Nun* gag." But she identifies with the passion of *Norma Rae* (far right).

"I was always determined to be the greatest athlete who ever lived," said Babe (clockwise from top left: hurling the javelin for 1932 Olympic gold; winning her first tennis tourney in 1946; showing the form that won three U.S. Opens; cuing up for pro billiards; being a world-record hurdler).

Babe Zaharias
She shattered preconceptions as well as athletic records

*I*N AN ERA WHEN WOMEN WERE MORE LIKELY TO WIELD BROOMS THAN BASEBALL BATS, MILDRED Didrikson Zaharias proved they could beat men at their own game—any game. Declining to "waste time with dolls," young "Babe" won her nickname by smacking home runs over the playground fence in her hometown of Beaumont, Texas. On the basketball court she once scored an astonishing 104 points in a game on her way to becoming an All-American—hailed by Grantland Rice as "the athletic phenomenon of all time, man or woman." Setting world records in hurdles, javelin and high jump, Babe struck gold twice in the 1932 Olympics. Next she transformed women's golf into a power game with her 250-yard drives, remarking, "It's not enough to swing at the ball. You've got to loosen your girdle and let the ball have it." While her true love was rumored to be another golfer on the tour, Babe stayed devoted to husband-manager George Zaharias, an affable, 296-pound ex-wrestler, who encouraged her inspiring comeback at the 1954 U.S. Open (she won by 12 strokes) shortly after cancer surgery. When the disease claimed her two years later, at 45, President Eisenhower was the first of many to salute the gritty champion who "finally had to lose this last one of all her battles." ■

Wilma Rudolph
Just walking would have been triumph

*T*HOUGH WILMA RUDOLPH MANAGED TO survive bouts of scarlet fever, pneumonia and polio at age 4, doctors doubted she would walk again. Undeterred, her mother, Blanche, a domestic, made the 90-mile round trip from Clarksville, Tennessee, on her day off each week for several years so her daughter (the 20th of railroad porter Ed Rudolph's 22 children) could get treatment. Back home, Wilma doggedly practiced her first steps, and, at 11, astonished her parents by kicking off her orthopedic shoe to shoot hoops. At 16 she did the impossible: She won a bronze in the 400-meter relay in the 1956 Olympics. Four sum-

mers later, in Rome, the now-famous Black Gazelle became the first American woman to take three golds, anchoring the 400-meter relay team and winning the 100- and 200-meter dash. But a trip to the White House to meet President Kennedy did not lead to a storybook ending. There were no lucrative endorsement deals then for Olympic athletes, and the professional track tour didn't exist. Her two marriages didn't last, and she raised four children while working in a succession of unstimulating jobs—at one point she was rejected for a bank loan because of her color. Dauntless, she established the Wilma Rudolph Foundation and encouraged future Olympians (Jackie Joyner-Kersee called her "my idol"). At her death, from brain cancer at 54, in 1994, there was just one dream the child taunted for her limp had not fulfilled: "to be average," Wilma Rudolph once said wistfully, "to be normal." ■

"When I ran, I felt like a butterfly," said Rudolph (feted by her Tennessee hometown after her 1960 wins).

Julia Roberts

A Georgia peach became Hollywood's pretty woman

"JULIA'S SMILE IS LIKE A THOUSAND-watt bulb," says Dermot Mulroney, her costar in *My Best Friend's Wedding*. "There's nothing like it when she smiles and laughs. You can't help but be drawn into it." That smile, blinding us to the implausibilities of her prostitute's character in the 1990 movie *Pretty Woman*, melted a zillion hearts, got her a third Oscar nomination and helped make Roberts Hollywood's first $7 million actress. By then she had already made a number of films and even earned Oscar nominations for *Steel Magnolias* and *Mystic Pizza*. But it was that hooker-as-Cinderella role that planted Roberts permanently in the firmament.

Born in Smyrna, Georgia, to parents who once ran a workshop for actors and writers, she left the South to join her older sister Lisa and her brother, actor Eric Roberts, in New York City just three days after her high school graduation. Eric found Roberts her first job in film, in *Blood Red*, a picture that wasn't released until after she was established. There were missteps in her career (*Mary Reilly, I Love Trouble*) as well as in her romantic life. She became engaged to two of her early costars, Dylan McDermott from *Magnolias* and Kiefer Sutherland from *Flatliners*. She broke off both relationships and then surprised even the omnipresent media by marrying hip country star Lyle Lovett in 1993. The union lasted only 18 months, but the pair remain close. The one constant is her public appeal. "I'm sort of the everygirl in these movies," Roberts, 30, has reflected. Others see something more special and giving, an Audrey Hepburn-like quality in a young woman who, like Hepburn, has volunteered on behalf of the UN. "Just wait and see," says actor Rupert Everett. "When she's 50, she'll be scrubbing babies in Calcutta." ■

"It's kinda great being me," Roberts (in 1993) has said. **"I have a remarkable, spectacular, amazing life for which I am so grateful."**

Danny Thomas rejected her for his *Daddy* show, saying, "With a nose like yours, you don't look like you could belong to me."

Mary Tyler Moore
She gave TV a new female image

"WHO COULD TURN THE WORLD ON WITH HER SMILE?" WAS NOT A difficult musical question in the 1970s, when Mary Tyler Moore transformed TV's portrayal of women. In place of perfect housewife June Cleaver or a doting daughter like *My Little Margie* came Mary Richards, thirtysomething and pursuing a career rather than a man. But, for the beloved star of *The Mary Tyler Moore Show*, life wasn't always self-assured. Moore's childhood had little warmth: Her utilities-clerk father was a martinet who alienated Mary and drove her alcoholic mother to despair. The lonely child's love of "all forms of make-believe" led her into showbiz (she was the Happy Hotpoint Pixie) and to her fortuitous landing on *The Dick Van Dyke Show*. Her personal tally was seven Emmies and two divorces, from sales rep Richard Meeker, then from MTM Enterprises boss Grant Tinker; and her troubled 24-year-old son by Meeker accidentally killed himself in a tragedy eerily reminiscent of *Ordinary People* (which won her a 1980 Oscar nomination). To blot the pain, she'd gulp down margaritas, until she checked into the Betty Ford Center. But the gritty performer made it after all, marrying cardiologist Robert Levine, 17 years her junior in '83. Continuing to score in films like *Flirting with Disaster*, she's no longer so self-critical at 61, relaxing with MTM reruns like everyone else. "It's as though it's something I've never seen before," she says. "It's a wonderful show." ■

BillieJeanKing

Her legacy: big purses for women

WHEN HER FIREFIGHTER FATHER TOOK her to see her first ball game, "what struck me like a thunderbolt," recalled King, "was that there were no women on that baseball diamond." Her mother, an Avon lady and amateur swimmer, advised the young shortstop to take up a feminine sport like, well, tennis. Billie Jean Moffitt did exactly that and soon reported to her parents, "This is what I want to do with my life." She took free lessons from a parks department pro and walked four miles to school each day to develop her endurance. But the Long Beach, California, youngster had some rough moments pursuing what was then an elitist sport. At a Los Angeles tournament, the 11-year-old brown-bagged it alone while her wealthier opponents dined in the clubhouse; later she was left out of a team picture for wearing shorts instead of a tennis dress. The episode "turned me upside down," she said. She made up for it by turning her sport upside down when she co-founded the first pro women's tennis tour in 1970—the next year she became the first woman athlete to win $100,000 in a single year (in '97 tennis's Martina Hingis landed a record $3.4 million).

The aggressiveness that would win King six Wimbledon and four U.S. Open singles titles rankled hidebound Bobby Riggs, who had won Wimbledon in 1939. The self-proclaimed "male-chauvinist pig" hustled the 29-year-old into a match at the Houston Astrodome in 1973. A TV audience of 60 million—plus a capacity crowd of 30,000—watched King (so nervous she threw up before the match) score a symbolic victory as she thrashed the braying, 55-year-old bully. It made her the world's most famous female athlete. But later publicity was not as welcome. In 1981 her lover Marilyn Barnett, a former hairdresser, outed King in a palimony suit over the Malibu beach house they had shared for seven years while the tennis star was still married to business manager Larry King (the couple had wed in 1965). Billie Jean lost fans—and endorsements. It took time, but her fans settled down and so did she. Her competitive juices still flow as coach of the U.S. Fed Cup team, cheering on the women who owe their popularity, and sizable paychecks, to her. ■

"Maybe it means people will start to respect women athletes," said King after whipping Bobby Riggs in the "battle of the sexes."

Since this glistening 1992 shot, she has played pro basketball and now, at 36, coaches kids in the inner city of her youth, works as a sports agent and hopes to start a family.

JackieJoyner-Kersee *A superjock outran the odds*

IN THE FAMILY'S RUNDOWN HOUSE IN crime-ridden East St. Louis, Illinois, her older brother Al Joyner remembered "Jackie and me crying together . . . swearing that someday we were going to make it." Their family had encouraged the notion. Her grandmother picked the name Jacqueline in 1962, "because someday this girl will be first lady of something." Their mother, a nurse's assistant who married at 16 (her husband was 14) and quickly had four children, wouldn't let Jackie date until she was 18. Instead, the girl shot milk-crate hoops with Al and trained for track by leaping over potato-chip bags filled with sand.

She had one pair of athletic shoes in high school, but they helped carry her team to state track and basketball championships. At UCLA, assistant track coach Bob Kersee took her on, recalling, "I saw this talent walking around the campus that everyone was blind to." She clearly clicked with the driven disciplinarian: He trained her to six medals in four Olympics, and they got (and stayed) married. (Brother Al also won a gold in the triple jump in 1984.) After Jackie had taken her gold in the 1992 heptathlon, in Barcelona, decathlete Bruce Jenner came onto the track to tell her she was "the greatest athlete who ever lived, male or female." ■

Ella Fitzgerald

From mean streets she bloomed as a blithe spirit

SHE ENTERED A TALENT CONTEST IN 1934 AS A DANCER AT Harlem's Apollo Theater but got cold feet, so to speak, and blurted out the song "The Object of My Affection" instead, winning the $25 first prize and a job with bandleader Chick Webb. In 1938, at 21, she presented him with the million-selling "A-Tisket, A-Tasket." "Not bad," Ella Fitzgerald would later judge her six-decade, 13-Grammy career, "for someone who only studied music to get that half credit in high school." She never graduated. Fitzgerald's mother had died when Ella was 15, and when her stepfather abused her, she moved in with an impoverished aunt in Harlem. Dropping out of school to run numbers on the street and work as a lookout for sporting houses, she landed in an Upstate New York reformatory. Not permitted to join its all-white choir, she "sang her heart out" at a nearby church, recalls a parishioner, just one year before her breakthrough at the Apollo. In the '40s, Ella took scatting to new levels of art in Dizzy Gillespie's band and later set the standard for standards in her composers' songbook series (while raising her son after both marriages failed). Yet the shy singer was as modest as her schoolmarm mien, often remarking before gigs, "I hope the people like me." They adored her. When the diabetes that forced the amputation of her legs killed her in 1996, at 79, Mel Torme called her "the best singer on the planet." ■

"I loved an audience from the time I could walk," said Wynette (in 1977). And the feeling was mutual: She sold more than 30 million copies of her 50 albums and ran 39 Top 10 hits up the country charts.

"Listening to Dizzy [with her in 1947] made me want to try something with my voice that would be like a horn," Ella said about scatting.

Tammy Wynette

The Queen of Country experienced every cotton-picking word she sang

YOU REALLY HAVE TO LIVE A COUNTRY SONG TO sing a country song. And with hardscrabble roots, and her dreams of stardom thwarted by the reality of being a young and divorced mother, Virginia Wynette Pugh sang with the heartbreaking twang that only experience provides. After her father's death, from a brain tumor when she was 9 months old, Virginia grew up picking cotton on her grandparents' Mississippi farm. Her first marriage ended after six years, while she was pregnant with her third child. Enrolling in beauty school, Wynette got a $30 gig singing on morning TV and moved to Nashville, where a record producer heard her, loved her and renamed her for a Debbie Reynolds film series. Her first single, "Apartment #9," was a hit, and bigger ones

("Stand by Your Man" and "D-I-V-O-R-C-E") followed in 1968. Though by then a star, Wynette kept bolls of cotton in a crystal dish to remind her of her roots.

Even with fame, her life played like a weepy ballad. She divorced three more husbands, including singer George Jones, who would get high and once chased her with a rifle. She found lasting love only with manager George Richey, in 1978. After suffering intestinal ailments, and undergoing 17 major surgeries that hooked her on painkillers, Wynette died at 55, in 1998, from a blood clot in her lung—but not before inspiring countless country artists with her story and her song. "I don't think she ever got over her ascendancy from the beauty parlor," said Rosanne Cash. "She was a vehicle for her voice, and it seemed to have ambition of its own." ∎

N

otorious

Joan Crawford

She strove to be a legend and became one—for all the wrong reasons

FORGET, IF IT'S POSSIBLE, WHAT YOU THINK OF JOAN Crawford—Faye Dunaway, in painted eyebrows arching like a cat, wielding a wire hanger over her cowering daughter. Before she was known as the worst stepmother since Snow White's, Crawford was an actress of notable, if unsubtle, talent and tenacity. After she'd appeared in silent and talkie pictures for a decade and MGM had renewed her $1.5 million contract, she was among the targets in an ad placed by moviehouse owners "tired of losing money on the glamour stars detested by the public." Ouch. Like characters she played—usually gritty, take-charge women—she turned her fate around. In 1946, Crawford became the first actor to hire a publicist to campaign for an Oscar—and won for *Mildred Pierce.* She was born Lucille LeSueur to a strict, unmarried mother. As a teen she parlayed a prize won in a Charleston contest into Broadway chorus work. She became Hollywood royalty, marrying Douglas Fairbanks Jr.; and after their divorce she wed actors Franchot Tone, Phillip Terry and Pepsi-Cola mogul Alfred N. Steele, while enjoying affairs with Clark Gable and Spencer Tracy. But men's love never meant as much to Crawford as that of her fans, for whom she would do anything, including, alleges daughter Christina, adopting four children to make her appear more sympathetic. After she died alone of a heart attack at age 69, her star remained untarnished for just one year before Christina published *Mommie Dearest,* the book that—more so than five decades of credits—ensured, and sullied, her mother's place in history. ■

Christina (with Mommie and brother Christopher) said discipline included being tied to the bed.

"Stanny White was killed," Nesbit said after her husband, 'Mad Harry' Thaw, shot the architect at Madison Square Garden, which he had designed. "But my fate was worse. I lived."

Evelyn Nesbit

For a skyscraping genius she proved a literal femme fatale

IN 1901 THE RUBY-LIPPED INNOCENT from Pittsburgh was dubbed Girl Model of Gotham and won a Broadway role. Her ethereal beauty bewitched the flamboyant Beaux-Arts architect Stanford White, who introduced her to haute society, established the showgirl, with her widowed seamstress mother, in plush digs—and invited her to his apartment to use a red-velvet swing, preferably naked. "Don't forget," she told a reporter later, "I was only 16, and I enjoyed swinging."

But with no proposal from White, Nesbit began to entertain other wealthy suitors. "Mad Harry" Thaw—heir to a $40-million railroad fortune and known for antics like trying to ride a horse into the elegant Union Club—piqued Evelyn's interest by sending her red roses wrapped in $50 bills. She described him as "a mighty peculiar person" but married him, in 1905, even though he had whipped her the year before when she told him about her prior relationship with White. "I was so sorry for him," she said. "And . . . we'd been so terribly poor." But Thaw's rage festered (he'd long held a grudge against White for blackballing him from exclusive clubs). Still steaming in 1906, Thaw pulled a pistol and killed White at a cabaret performance. The "trial of the century" produced a hung jury; in a retrial, Thaw was found not guilty by reason of insanity. After his release from a prison for the criminally insane, in 1915, Thaw divorced Nesbit. She struggled as a vaudeville dancer and attempted suicide twice. Nesbit finally found peace teaching sculpture in California and looked back fondly at her first love. "Stanford White," she said before she died in 1967, at 82, "was the

McPherson (in a 1935 pageant) was fictionalized in *Elmer Gantry* by Sinclair Lewis and portrayed in the film version by Jean Simmons.

Aimee Semple McPherson

She sold salvation with a flamboyant showbiz spin

JESUS IS COMING SOON: GET READY!" SO WARNED THE BANner on the side of Aimee Semple McPherson's "gospel car." Driving cross-country with her mother (likely the first women to travel extensively by auto unaccompanied by a man), "Sister Aimee" led revivals in the 1920s and ultimately settled in Los Angeles to found a new denomination, the Church of the Foursquare Gospel. There the once-widowed and twice-divorced mother of two built a 5,000-member congregation upon the twin attractions of Pentecostalism—which included speaking in tongues and being "slain in the Holy Spirit"—and show business, using elaborate sets and costumes on the pulpit.

Born in Ontario to a farmer and a Salvation Army member, she became the first public figure to use radio for sermons and healing. But McPherson was criticized for the contradiction between what she preached, total devotion to God, and how she lived—with seeming devotion to money and her own happiness, tossing off two husbands who cramped her career. Well before her 1944 death (at age 54, of an accidental sleeping-pill overdose), her church sold cemetery space near her plot with the slogan: "Go Up with Aimee." ■

"Holdups were things Bonnie never really did get to care for," said Clyde, contradicting legend.

Bonnie Parker

Shooting and looting, Clyde's sweetheart did it all for love

NOTHING IN BONNIE PARKER'S VERY SHORT LIFE INFURIATED HER MORE THAN THE 1933 photo taken in Joplin, Missouri, that depicted her as the tough, stogie-puffing gun moll of the Barrow gang ("Tell them," she would say, "I don't smoke cigars!"). Bonnie still saw herself as the sensitive young girl who longed to escape dusty Rowena, Texas—where she was already famous as the city's spelling champ—to become a poet, a singer or an actress (an elocution coach said she had a talent for theatrics). But opportunity was limited during the Depression, and the appealing five-foot strawberry blonde found herself chasing tips as a waitress. She finally broke free by marrying the devilishly handsome—and criminally inclined—Roy Thornton, who was soon taken from their home to the big house. While Thornton was doing life for murder, Bonnie became smitten with another rogue, Clyde Barrow. Soon she had all the drama she craved as the reckless pair embarked on a two-year criminal and romantic odyssey that left 10 lawmen dead and put the country into a panic.

Ever loyal to the one man who had never left her, Bonnie refused a police offer of freedom for betraying Clyde—even though Clyde had begged her to save herself. "When he dies, I want to die anyway," she told her mother a year before they were both gunned down by sheriffs, she at 23, in Gibland, Louisiana. That was in 1934, after the once-hopeful poet had finished the immortalizing work that became the germ of a major motion picture: *The Ballad of Bonnie and Clyde*. ∎

Ma Barker

Life on the lam and death were her family values

IN THE DEPTHS OF THE DEPRESSION, ARIzona Donnie Barker became the matriarch of American crime, a woman whose gritty legend spread like a dust bowl tornado. Leaving her husband, George, behind in the Ozarks, Ma, as she was known, and her gang, including her three desperado sons, terrorized the Midwest from 1931 to 1935 with a string of spectacular kidnappings, robberies and murders. Little is known about the woman behind the icon except that she was a blindly devoted mom. One former member of the so-called Bloody Barkers said that Ma was so ignorant, "she couldn't plan breakfast." But J. Edgar Hoover wrote that she had masterminded the gang's activities, quoting her as boasting, " 'I got great days ahead of me when my children grow up. Fur coats and diamond rings.' " Always on the run, the Barkers had no chance to enjoy their swag. Ma's son Doc Barker was killed in an attempted escape from Alcatraz, and his brother Herman shot himself when cornered by police. Ma and Fred were killed, in 1935, at a Florida resort town in an epic, four-hour shootout with the FBI. Their bodies were left in a morgue for 10 months before George Barker could scratch up the money to bury his wife and son. ∎

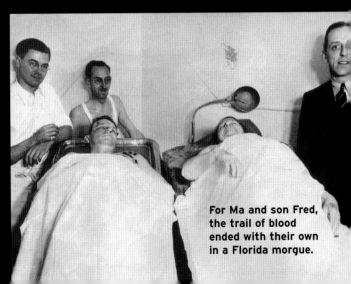

For Ma and son Fred, the trail of blood ended with their own in a Florida morgue.

Mata Hari

She played a deadly game of kiss and tell

A S AN EXOTIC DANCER IN PRE-WW I PARIS, Mata Hari ("eye of the morning") claimed to be the daughter of an Indian princess, but Margaretha Zeele MacLeod (born in 1876) was actually sired by a Dutch hatmaker. She fled to Paris at 30 following personal disasters: Her son was poisoned by his nanny, and she lost custody of her daughter after divorcing her philandering husband. In the Great War, the Germans paid her for passing on classified pillow talk, but the aging courtesan turned out to be rather inept as a spy. Learning she had joined French counterintelligence, the Germans probably set up agent "H21" so the French would discover her duplicity. Mata Hari was executed by firing squad in 1917. Many thought the French had used her as a scapegoat to distract from their huge losses on the western front. ■

An ANC lawyer called Winnie (with husband Nelson, left, in 1992) "bloody ambitious."

Winnie Mandela

A freedom fighter lost her compass

S HE WAS A 22-YEAR-OLD STUNNER WHEN she met African National Congress leader Nelson Mandela in 1956. Six years after they married, he was sentenced to life in prison for antiapartheid activities. During his 27-year confinement, government officials harassed Winnie continually: She was held in solitary for 18 months, without charges, and banished to a remote house without running water. Radicalized, she retaliated by spurring her supporters to terrorism. Her patriotism earned her the sobriquet Mother of the Nation. But when her personal goon squad kidnapped four black youngsters she suspected of being police informers and killed a 14-year-old, in 1988, Winnie was dubbed Mugger of the Nation. (She was convicted as an accessory to assault in 1991, but her sentence was reduced to a fine.) In 1996, a year after her attacks on the government forced the president to oust her from his cabinet, she and Mandela divorced. ■

Imelda Marcos

An ex-beauty queen funded her shopping sprees with the state budget

GROWING UP IN A SMALL PHILIPPINE VILLAGE, IMELDA ROMUALDEZ ONCE SAID SHE ASPIRED ONLY to "a tiny little house with a little picket fence and a little car. That would be enough." Of course, it turned out to be not nearly enough for this poor cousin of a wealthy clan. When, as a 25-year-old beauty queen, she married then-Congressman Ferdinand Marcos—the two had first met when he spoke at her high school graduation—she couldn't wait to play catch-up. Becoming a world-class shopper, she helped President Marcos loot the country of literally billions during a corrupt, 20-year rule. When finally run out of Manila, in 1986, the couple moved operations to Honolulu, where a supportive U.S. government granted them lavish asylum. Ferdinand died in Hawaii in 1989, but in 1991, at 62, Imelda returned, like MacArthur, to the Philippines (where she was reunited with 1,220 pairs of shoes she'd left in Malacañang Palace). There she faced fraud and racketeering charges—and ran for president as "mother of the nation." She didn't win. But she did, as promised, make a contribution to her country: She auctioned off her famous shoe collection to benefit the poor. ∎

"Before," said Marcos after being booted out of her country, "I was Imelda the First Lady. Now I am Imelda the deprived, the crucified." (Back in Manila, in 1992, she paid respects at a bust of Ferdinand.)

Ingrid Bergman

She followed
her heart and caused
an international incident

In Rome, in 1956,
Bergman played house
for the cameras with
inamorato Roberto
Rossellini.

IN THE MOVIES SHE OFTEN PLAYED A SAINT: JOAN OF ARC, IN A FILM OF THAT NAME, OR A nun in *The Bells of Saint Mary's*. But in 1950, Ingrid Bergman was, at least according to one moralizing U.S. senator, "a powerful influence for evil." She had already been a beloved star in her native Sweden and in Hollywood for many years, gracing pictures like *Intermezzo* and *Casablanca*, but when she became pregnant by her lover, the Italian director Roberto Rossellini, before getting a divorce from her first husband, Swedish physician Petter Lindstrom, the industry blacklisted Bergman. That senator, Edward Johnson, proposed licenses for actors that could be revoked if they behaved as sinfully as he felt Bergman had. (He also had a few words for RKO pictures, which exploited the scandal to promote Rossellini's first film with Bergman, *Stromboli*.) Once her divorce came through, she wed Rossellini, gave birth to a son, Robertino, and later to twin daughters, Ingrid and Isabella. The marriage lasted only two years, during which time Bergman was unable to see her first daughter, Pia, who had remained with her father. She later married and divorced Lars Schmidt, a Swedish producer.

But as she proved herself a good mother to her children, Bergman regained the hearts of many who had been judgmental, and was allowed to make an American comeback in *Anastasia*, for which she won the second of her three Oscars. Her movie roles were fewer later in life, when Bergman suffered from breast cancer and underwent two mastectomies. The year before her death, at age 67, she came out of retirement to play Golda Meir in a television film, for which she won an Emmy. In a 1980 interview, Bergman recalled, "When I was very young in Sweden, I used to pray, 'God, please don't let me have a dull life.' He obviously heard me." ∎

Ayn Rand

This cult philosopher believed money was the root of all good

AN HAUTE BOURGEOIS CHILDHOOD spent in tattered Leningrad after the Revolution convinced Alice Rosenbaum that Communism was soul-destroying. She sailed for America at 21 and eventually took the name Ayn (to sound like *ein*, the German word for "one") and Rand (from the typewriter she used to punch out screenplays in Hollywood). Her worship of laissez-faire capitalism and rampant individualism led to a philosophy called objectivism that she peddled in two epic, mega-selling novels, *The Fountainhead* (later a movie with Gary Cooper) and *Atlas Shrugged*. Impressed by a fan letter from Nathaniel Branden, a grad student 25 years her junior, she anointed him as her "intellectual heir," and the pair—though both married—began a long affair. When Branden left her because of her age, the vainglorious Rand, then 63, said he should prefer her "above any woman on earth even if I were 80 and in a wheelchair." Though once called "one of the truly impossible people of all time," she became a lecture-circuit cult figure. When Rand died at 77, in 1982, a bouquet shaped like a dollar sign towered over her coffin. ∎

Her captors issued this propaganda placard of Patty as "Tania" in 1974.

Patty Hearst

A San Simeon heir turned Symbionese Army poster girl

THE PHOTOS WERE BLURRED AND jerky—ghostly gray figures caught on a surveillance camera at San Francisco's Hibernia Bank on an April afternoon in 1974. But there was no denying the identity of one of the robbers: Kidnapped newspaper heiress Patty Hearst, 20, a carbine propped on her hip, stood guard while members of the self-styled Symbionese Liberation Army grabbed cash from frightened tellers.

Two months earlier, SLA radicals had dragged Hearst, screaming, from her Berkeley, California, apartment at gunpoint and subjected her to 57 days of rape and torture. She later claimed, in her only discussion of her complicity in the crime, that she had thought her captors would kill her if she did not go along. At her 1975 trial, Hearst's attorneys compared her actions to those of prisoners of war brainwashed by their captors. But at the time, Hearst seemed a willing convert, savagely denouncing Steven Weed, the boyfriend she had been living with, and taking the nom-de-revolution Tania. When cap-tured by the FBI after 17 months on the lam, she raised a clenched fist in defiance. A victim turned villain in the public mind, the convent-educated child of privilege had become an ironic symbol of the era's dying counterculture.

Sentenced to seven years in prison for armed robbery, Hearst served 22½ months before President Jimmy Carter commuted her sentence in February 1979. Two months later, Hearst wed San Francisco police sergeant Bernard Shaw, 53, who had been her bodyguard while she was free on bond. Now the mother of two daughters (Gillian, 16, and Lydia, 12), Hearst, 44, lives in Connecticut, makes the Manhattan social scene and dabbles in both writing (including her 1982 autobiography and a 1996 mystery novel, *Murder at San Simeon*) and acting (*Cry-Baby*, *Serial Mom*). "I'm just seizing control of my reputation," she told *The New York Times* in 1996. "I find it strange for people to think that after being kidnapped, I should remain in hiding for the rest of my life." ■

Her fiancé, Bernard Shaw, joined Hearst at her 1979 release.

Angela Davis

Black was beautiful—and defiant—as embodied by this radical professor

ER VISAGE ON COUNTLESS DORM-ROOM posters—fist raised, defiance radiating from an awesomely intimidating Afro—made Angela Davis a prime symbol of the Black Power struggle. To the political left, she was the cause's Carrie Nation; to conservatives, a virulent subversive. Alabama-raised, she attended Brandeis and did her junior year at the Sorbonne. "Her beauty was so striking," a classmate later recalled, "that men followed her and stumbled over each other to light her cigarettes." Davis ignored them and fell in with Algerian revolutionaries at the cafés. In the turbulent '60s she became a brilliant young philosophy professor at UCLA, a card-carrying Communist and, briefly, a Black Panther.

Davis might have remained just another campus radical had she not headed a movement to free the Soledad Brothers, four black convicts at a Northern California penitentiary. She wrote passionate letters to their leader, George Jackson, but met him only a few times—in prison visiting rooms. Then, on August 7, 1970, using a pistol he had stolen from Davis, Jackson's younger brother Jonathan took hostages in the Marin County courtroom in an attempt to negotiate his brother's freedom. Jonathan

Jackson and two others, including the judge, were killed in a hail of gunfire. Because her gun was used, the FBI put Davis on its Most Wanted list. She fled but was later arrested for murder and conspiracy, spending 16 months in jail. After a three-month-long trial in 1972, she was acquitted of all charges.

In the interim, however, "Free Angela!" had entered the aural history of the counterculture. Now 54 and a feminist-studies professor at the University of California, Santa Cruz, Davis still crusades for prison reform as well as for gay rights. She came out publicly as a lesbian in 1993 but adamantly refuses to discuss personal subjects. Looking back on her sensational hour in the public eye, she said, "It was hard having my whole political life reduced to a hairdo. I was basically an Afro, not a person." ∎

In 1970, Davis posed after being fired from UCLA under pressure from then Governor Ronald Reagan.

Jean Harris

A well-bred headmistress committed an infamous crime of passion

WHEN SHE MET DR. HERMAN Tarnower, creator of the celebrated Scarsdale Diet, Jean Harris had long been out of an unhappy marriage and reserved her passion for her career as headmistress of the exclusive Madeira School in McLean, Virginia. But the woman her students called Integrity Harris soon became obsessed with her lover. Over the course of their 14-year affair, her self-respect was consistently undermined by Tarnower's unfaithfulness (he carried on with some 30 women) and a broken date at the altar. Then, when he took up with his new young assistant Lynne Tryforos, the vulnerable, 56-year-old schoolmarm finally cracked: She drove to Tarnower's house, pulled out a .32-caliber revolver and shot him dead. Though many sympathized, she was sentenced, in 1981, to 15 years for second-degree murder.

When she arrived at Bedford Hills maximum-security prison, north of New York City, Harris, said author Shana Alexander, "just cried all the time." But slowly she began to adjust and even to thrive, writing three books about prison life. Despite ill health—she suffered three heart attacks in her 12 years there—she marshaled her waning strength and long experience in education to help the inmates she had grown to respect ("I know a hundred women who make Job look like a crybaby," she once remarked). Harris taught parenting classes (her own two sons visited her in prison faithfully) and cared for inmates' children in the prison nursery. Three hours before she underwent quadruple-bypass surgery, in December 1992, New York Governor Mario Cuomo accepted her fourth plea for clemency. Shortly afterward, Harris retired to a log cabin in Monroe, New Hampshire, where once again the now 74-year-old schoolteacher helps mold young people's lives, this time through a foundation—established with the earnings of her books—that funds private school education for children of Bedford Hills inmates.

Dogged by the media, the defendant kept her dignity during her murder trial and the long internment thereafter.

Fergie

She knew she was unsuited for royalty, but it was a fun (if bumpy) ride while it lasted

"I wouldn't change a day of it," swore Fergie (in 1990) of her days of infamy. Not even the "hellish day" in 1992 when she was snapped topless by the British tabs with her toe-kissing lover and "felt like Eve fallen from grace."

I T WAS DREADFUL," SAID SARAH FERGUSON, PUTTING HER SPIN ON THE ROYAL FAMILY'S chagrined view of her 10-year marriage to Andrew, Duke of York. "They tried to put the little redhead in a cage." The Windsors probably didn't know what they were getting into when they seated the daughter of Prince Charles's polo manager next to the Queen's second son at an Ascot luncheon. Neither did Fergie. She and Andy flirted, and a year later, in 1986, they wed. At first she was popular—more so, said some observers, than Princess Diana. But soon the Palace wanted to muzzle her. (When an admirer called to her from a crowd, Fergie winked and called back, "I'll see *you* later.") Gaining weight, she was dubbed Duchess of Pork by the press, which ran unflattering pictures of her ungainly thigh-flashing exits from limos. Fergie trysted with American financial advisor John Bryan and landed in the tabs topless in 1992, in vacation photos that showed him kissing her toes as her two young daughters looked on. She and Andrew divorced in 1996. But the Duchess kept living large, accruing $2.3 million in debt, and began doing paid commercial endorsements. Signing on as a million-dollar spokeswoman for Weight Watchers in 1997, Fergie said, "I don't want to pay the price of being overweight again . . . I've already paid some awfully high prices for the sins of my life." ∎

Roseanne

Chewing up hubbies and middle-class mores served her splendor in the crass

M ORE AIR-RAID SIREN THAN SEDUCTIVE siren, Roseanne nonetheless lured zillions of TV viewers into her tattered den of domestic hell. Her couch-potato Conner clan weren't the first to loosen their blue collars in prime time, but none had done so with such defiant, lowbrow chauvinism. "The series," wrote *The New York Times*, "played a crucial role in defining social class and establishing the dysfunctional family as the norm in the 1990s." Dysfunction has always been the curdled mother's milk of Roseanne's comedy. In her early stand-up days in Denver, she skewered husbands who mistook their wives for homing devices when they wanted to find the bag of Cheetos: "Like *he* couldn't go over and lift up the sofa cushions himself?" In two bestselling books, Roseanne flaunted her seamy and strident past: A Jewish girl from Mormon Salt Lake City, she alleged that both her mother and father had molested her as a child; and she confessed she had supplemented waitressing wages with prostitution, and had given up a daughter for adoption. A nose job and lavish living eventually detached Roseanne from what she had proudly called her "working-class" roots. As if liposuctioned, her audience evaporated too. ∎

When her "Star-Spangled" yammer was booed at a San Diego Padres game (in 1990), Roseanne gave a rude riposte.

Funny LADIES

Lucille BALL

*One syndicated
sensation, she is
the female clown
of the century*

A LEGGY EX-MODEL FROM UPSTATE NEW YORK, Lucille Ball said she "never cared much for movies" or the tough-talking glamor queens she played for two decades: "They cast me wrong." So with the dawn of the TV age, Ball shrewdly recast herself into a comedian brave enough to battle pigeons on a ledge while dressed as Superman, or face a hideous, hilarious death from an expanding loaf of bread. "From that talent came the greatest creation in television history—Lucy," observes a colleague in the medium. "In many respects, Lucille Ball made TV by giving real style and dimension to the genre we now call the sitcom." The admiring colleague is Mary Tyler Moore. *I Love Lucy*, the favorite sitcom of all time and likely to remain so, in reruns, was rated No. 1 in four of its six seasons (1951 to 1957). That the husband was played by Ball's real-life mate, Desi Arnaz, a Cuban-born bandleader turned shrewd boss of Desilu Productions, brought the series closer to every home except, ironically, their own. "Lucy solved a lot of marital problems for our viewers," said Ball in 1961, "and the idea of finding a laugh in a hopeless situation worked for Desi and me a long time." Yet Arnaz's drinking and philandering had forced Ball to divorce the father of her two kids and the man intimates called "the one great love of her life." Eighteen months after her 1960 divorce, she settled in for keeps with comedian Gary Morton. The public mourned when Ball, 77, died of a ruptured aorta in 1989. As Walter Matthau had said, "They liked Ike, but they loved Lucy." ∎

Lucy (cavorting with Vivian Vance in 1952) turned slapstick into art.

Though she made funny business seem effortless, Ball was a self-confessed work-aholic. After she bought out Desi's interest in their studio, in 1962, for $2.5 million, she joked, "Up until now I have been vice president in charge of dusting. Now I'll have to sweep up too."

The original Funny Girl lovingly stood by her scoundrel

Fanny BRICE

LET THE WORLD know you as you are, not as you think you should be," said Fanny Brice. "Because sooner or later, if you are posing, you will forget the pose, and then where are you?" As a teenager the former Fannie Borach, of New York City's Lower East Side, was keen to let the world see her as she was— skinny, beaky, gawky—and talented. Funny, with a big voice, she took the stage at amateur nights and small burlesque houses, where, in 1910, she was discovered by Florenz Ziegfeld, who offered her $75 a week to appear in his famous *Follies*. The daughter of a saloon-keeper father and a mother who worked in the *schmatte* trade, Brice graced both stage and radio with memorable songs ("Second-Hand Rose") and characters (Baby Snooks, a bratty child known for her trademark whine: "Why, Daddy?"). Besides doing comedy she could sing a ballad with the best. Her theme song became "My Man," a bittersweet irony because the man in her life, Nicky Arnstein, was nothing but trouble. But she stood by the gambler and con man, selling her jewels to pay his lawyers and sticking with him throughout his prison sentence for embezzling millions from Wall Street. Asked how she could love a man like that, Brice replied, "With my heart," a tragicomic quip repeated by Barbra Streisand when she played Brice onstage and in film in *Funny Girl*. After her divorce from Arnstein, Brice married producer Billy Rose, who left her for a champion swimmer. She died, at 59, after a stroke, with her son and daughter from her marriage to Arnstein at her side. "When love is out of your life," Brice once noted, "you're through in a way." ∎

"Love is like a card trick," said Brice (at a 1939 birthday party). **"Once you learn how it's done, you can't be fooled any longer."**

Gracie ALLEN

George lived a century but never met another Gracie

ALL I HAD TO DO WAS STAND next to her and imagine some of the applause was for me," said George Burns fondly of his partner in love and laughter. The two vaudevillians teamed up in 1922, first with Allen, 18, as the straight man and Burns, 27, hitting the punch lines. Delivered in a chirpy, spacey voice, Allen's set-ups almost always won more laughs than his payoffs—so they swapped roles. George: "Did something happen to you as a baby?" Gracie: "When I was born, I was so surprised, I couldn't talk for a year and a half." The formula served them for 40 years as a comedy team on stage, radio, film and television.

Performing in her father's musical revues from age 3, Allen was nothing like her loopy, onstage personality. She was shy, particularly about a disfiguring burn on one arm, the result of a childhood accident. Devoted as wife, mother and friend ("She was the first person I would go to when I had a problem," said fellow comedian Mary Livingstone), Allen was resilient as well. After the one occasion when Burns had been unfaithful, he apologized by giving her a lavish gift. Later Allen joked, "I wish George would find another girlfriend—I could use a silver-fox jacket." Gracie retired in 1958 to spend more time with her two children and grandchildren. Just six years later, after suffering multiple heart attacks, she died, at 58. Burns's career would bloom again years later, but he never remarried. "My life," he said, even three decades after her death, "was Gracie." ∎

Marry me, or I'll break up the act, is more or less how Burns proposed to Allen. (In 1935 they celebrated July 4th, Gracie-style.)

POWDER

"When a woman goes wrong, men go right after her," cracked West (in 1940, with Edgar Bergen and bodice-gripper Charlie McCarthy).

Goldie HAWN

The '60s 'dumb blonde' plays it smart in the '90s

F OR THE MOMENT, THE trademark giggle was gone. "I'm smarter than people give me credit for," stated Goldie Hawn during a 1997 self-assessment. "I have a light personality and a deep-thinking brain."

Believe her. Using the latter, Hawn has parlayed the former—what she calls her "zany-ditsy-dingy shtick"—into one of Hollywood's most beloved and powerful careers. Her joie de vivre came with her genes. Born near Washington to a musician father and a mother who ran a jewelry business and dancing school, "I have always possessed a certain joy," Hawn says. Dropping out of college, she go-go danced in New York City and Las Vegas before making her delightfully birdbrained entrance, in 1968, on *Rowan & Martin's Laugh-In*. The next year, Hawn was also an Oscar winner, for her role as a kooky salesgirl in *Cactus Flower*. With the $100-million success of 1980's *Private Benjamin*, Hawn's first of many forays as a producer, "it was time," she says, "for me to become a businesswoman."

Hawn's marriage to second husband Bill Hudson failed in 1980, and in a bitter divorce she won custody of son Oliver, now 22, and daughter Kate, 19, both actors. Three years later the poorly received *Swing Shift* paired her and Kurt Russell, with whom Hawn has lived, unwed, for 15 years (and with whom she has a son, Wyatt, 12). "Marriage is a form of ownership," the free spirit has said of remarrying. "I don't like fusion. I think it's dangerous. You lose personal power." At 52, Goldie is in no danger of sacrificing her own. ■

Jail couldn't blunt her broad humor Mae WEST

S OME HAVE CALLED MADONNA THE MAE WEST OF TODAY. BUT West took more risks. After she peeved censors with her ribald humor, she spent 10 days behind bars. The Brooklyn-born daughter of a former prizefighter and a corset model, West started as a singer with a gift for improv and turned to playwrighting in 1926. Her first legitimate play, bluntly called *Sex*, was an Off-Broadway hit despite newspapers' refusing its ads. The censors noticed it too: West was charged with corrupting "the morals of youth and others," fined and thrown in the clink for those 10 days. Her next play, *The Pleasure Man*, got the whole cast arrested, but no one was jailed. The incidents didn't hurt West's career. At 40, she moved to Hollywood. Her work (with curmudgeonly pal W.C. Fields and newcomer Cary Grant) led to the sudden enforcement of the Motion Picture Production Code, which regulated morality in films till the 1960s. West died, at 87, having proved the truth of one of her favorite lines: "It's better to be looked-over than overlooked." ■

On *Rowan & Martin's Laugh-In*, the camera would zoom in on a topically tattooed Hawn (in '68), who would stop her gyrating just long enough to be read.

Lily TOMLIN

Prune-faced operators and nasal tots festoon her fertile mind

WHEN MARY JEAN TOMLIN INVESTED THE PROFITS of her teenage babysitting in a set of magic tricks, she was warned by her family's genteel neighbor Mrs. Rupert, "If you're not careful, you're going to grow up and be in show business." Tomlin wasn't careful. The Detroit native later transformed Mrs. Rupert ("who wore gloves and fox furs and a hat with a veil to empty the garbage") into a character in her act. One of many.

Although Tomlin studied premed at Wayne State for two years (making her factory-worker father and home-maker mother proud), she soon relocated to Manhattan to raise her nascent gift for parody into what she called "guerrilla art." In 1969, Tomlin's quirky alter egos—like Edith Ann, the 6-year-old who delivers her nasal observations from an oversize rocking chair—helped make *Rowan & Martin's Laugh-In* a smash. Then she confounded Hollywood expectations by choosing the downbeat role of a jilted wife in Robert Altman's *Nashville* (and was rewarded with an Oscar nomination).

The population of the village between her ears continued to boom in Tomlin's Tony-winning, one-woman shows, *Appearing Nitely* and *The Search for Signs of Intelligent Life in the Universe* (cowritten with her longtime collaborator Jane Wagner). Here one met an insightful New York bag lady and a '60s activist trying to keep pace as an '80s superwoman. Tomlin didn't just tickle ribs; she needled them. Which is why even a certified cynic like Richard Pryor called her a "goddamn national treasure." At 59, Tomlin still appears on TV (PBS kids' shows and late of *Murphy Brown*) and the screen (*Krippendorf's Tribe*), not letting that treasure molder in the vault. ■

"We don't listen. We don't have to. We're the phone company," the snide Ernestine (circa 1972) reminded hapless customers on *Rowan & Martin's Laugh-In.*

*Her slapstick soul
(and great gams) brought
back a little bit of Lucy*

Carol BURNETT

WHETHER SHE WORE A DRESS MADE of velvet drapes (complete with drapery rods) as Miss Starlet in a send-up of *Gone with the Wind,* or sported NFL shoulder pads as Joan Crawford in "Mildred Fierce," Carol Burnett stopped at nothing in pursuit of a laugh. For one thing, she felt she owed her grandmother nothing less. It was Mae White who raised her in a seedy Hollywood boardinghouse after Carol's alcoholic parents turned their backs on her. She and "Nanny" took in about six movies a week. In the silvery flicker she saw that "there were always happy endings." So, she wondered, "why shouldn't I have a happy ending?"

Why not? At an acting class at UCLA, Burnett first realized she could make someone other than Nanny laugh. Her talent so impressed a benefactor (secret to this day) that he loaned her a thousand bucks to travel to New York City for her first audition.

After years of mugging for variety shows hosted by Ed Sullivan and Garry Moore, the comedian finally got her own gig, in 1967, with *The Carol Burnett Show.* It lasted 11 years and nabbed 25 Emmys. Each week, Burnett opened by tugging her ear, a special greeting to her grandmother.

Underneath the pratfalls, as with so many comics, pain lingered. Two marriages ended in divorce. Burnett felt that her parents' abandonment had instilled in her a reflexive hunger for approval and a timidity in personal relationships that she refers to as People Pleaser's Disease. Yet through the splits, and daughter Carrie's drug problems (now behind her), Burnett never lost pleasure in performing. Three years ago, at 62, she returned to the Broadway stage in the farce *Moon over Buffalo.* Not everyone loved it, but Burnett was unfazed. She had realized on her own show that "if you get 30 percent of the audience laughing, you're home-free." ■

"There are a lot of big egos in this business," said TV castmate Vicki Lawrence, "but that's not Carol's trip."

Whoopi GOLDBERG

*Politically incorrect
before it was cool to be
politically incorrect*

"I'm God's jester,"
Whoopi Goldberg
(in 1992) once
wisecracked, with
typical chutzpah.
"He puts me on his
shoulder to keep
him laughing."

W HETHER IT'S HER CHEEKY NAME, HER MEDUSAN DREADLOCKS, HER HIGH-BEAM GRIN OR her streetwise sass, Whoopi Goldberg has a knack for getting noticed. In 1983, Mike Nichols caught her wrenching, one-woman show—in which she conjured up hard-luck heartbreakers like Fontaine, a Harlem drug dealer who winds up weeping in Anne Frank's secret room—and moved the production uptown to Broadway, pronouncing her "one-part Elaine May, one-part Groucho Marx . . . and five-parts never seen before." Steven Spielberg then asked for a private performance (she tossed in an *ET* parody) and immediately cast her in *The Color Purple* as Celie, who surmounts poverty and abuse. Goldberg knows about starting the hard way. Raised in a New York City housing project, Caryn Johnson was a high school dropout and former junkie when she moved with her young daughter to San Diego in 1974. There the budding improv artist scraped by as a bricklayer, mortuary beautician ("they never complained about how they looked") and welfare recipient. "The *greatest* thing I ever was able to do," she has said, "was give a welfare check back. I brought it back to the welfare department and said, 'Here, I don't need this anymore.' " At first she billed herself as Whoopi Cushion, until her nurse mom said, "Nobody's going to respect you with a name like that." So, Whoopi has noted, "I put Goldberg on it. Goldberg's a part of my family, somewhere. . . ." Slowly the comedian built a movie career, overcoming resistance from the producers of 1990's *Ghost* who finally cast her as the psychic, a performance that won her a Best Supporting Actress Oscar. In 1997, she took over the lead in Broadway's *Forum* from Nathan Lane, transforming the role into a Whoopifest. Thrice-divorced, Goldberg, who is 48 and a grandmother, hasn't had any crystal balls in her love life. But with actor Frank Langella, she says, she is enjoying a romance that isn't just "a Band-Aid." ∎

Minnie PEARL

The tag on her hat read $1.98, but the cornpone was priceless

F OR MORE THAN HALF A CENTURY, SARAH Ophelia Colley Cannon marched out on the Grand Ole Opry stage and hollered, "Howdeee! I'm just so proud to be here!" Yet Cannon didn't in the least resemble her hayseed creation Minnie Pearl. The daughter of a Tennessee lumberman, she attended the tony Ward-Belmont College. But childhood acting dreams—"I didn't want to be a clown," she insisted, "I wanted to be Katharine Hepburn"—led her, at 21, to join a third-rate, traveling theatrical troupe. At one whistle-stop in Baileyton, Alabama, she bunked with a garrulous old mountain woman, who provided all the inspiration Cannon needed to devise one of the most memorable characters in the history of country music.

The hick humor of Minnie Pearl often focused on "ketchin' a feller." In 1947 she nabbed her own, Henry Cannon, an ex-pilot who flew her and other country stars to concert dates. When breast cancer caused her to have a double mastectomy, in 1985, she went public to give others courage—as she had when she comforted a heartbroken Opry crowd, in 1963, after the plane crash that killed Patsy Cline. A stroke took Cannon in 1996, at 83, but the giggle and the gingham linger on. ∎

Vintage Pearl: "Mrs. Tugwell just had her 16th young 'un . . . she's running out of names—to call her husband!"

Joan RIVERS

Gossipy, loud, catty (don't forget chic!), she gloried in girl talk

S HE NEVER ACTUALLY OCCUPIED "THE ENTIRE front row" in a class picture, as she later joked, but the insecurities that fueled her act were real enough. They were nurtured in her Brooklyn home by Russian-Jewish refugee parents whom she described as "almost pathologically terrified of poverty." Movie magazines painted life in rosier tones, so she sent her photo to MGM and entered a *Photoplay* acting contest, placing second. But a nice Jewish girl wants to please Mom, so Joan Rivers (née Molinsky) graduated from Barnard College (Phi Beta Kappa) and plied the rag trade as national fashion coordinator for a clothing chain, even marrying the boss's son.

It didn't last a year. Rivers renewed childhood acting dreams with Chicago's Second City comedy troupe, and an encounter with edgy comic Lenny Bruce inspired her intimate "Can we talk?" style. Audiences loved the way she skewered celebrities like Elizabeth Taylor ("Mosquitoes see her and scream, 'Buffet!' "). But, in 1987, her life was upended by the suicide of her husband of 22 years, Edgar Rosenberg, who was also her manager. Rivers blamed herself (as did daughter Melissa) for failing to help him deal with depression after his debilitating heart attack. The two have since patched up their relationship, and both work on E! network's *Fashion Reviews*. On Oscar night, Rivers, 65, lampooned the sartorial efforts of some of the nominees. "He got $12 million for his last movie," she sniffed. "You'd think he'd buy a decent tuxedo." ∎

Departing *Tonight* to host her own show, in 1986, Rivers (in '83) called herself "the only woman in the history of the world who left Johnny Carson and didn't ask him for money."

Sandra BERNHARD

Dahling, there's no biz like showbiz—especially to spoof without mercy

WITHOUT IRONY, SHE'S NOTHING. OR so she'd like you to think. Belting out a public persona framed in air quotes, Sandra Bernhard "sings," "acts" and "tells jokes." But for all her "I'm-not-really-doing-this-am-I?" distance, the truth is that she really can sing—everything from Burt Bacharach to Prince. She proved herself a fine actress in Martin Scorsese's *The King of Comedy.* And she's raucously funny in her one-woman shows, and as *Roseanne*'s bisexual pal on television. She mocks what she embraces.

You would have to have a sense of humor to be Bernhard. Her father is a proctologist; her mother, an abstract painter. She is genetically blessed with a supermodel's body but sees in the mirror each morning lips that rightly belong on Mick Jagger, not Christy Turlington. "I have one of those hard-to-believe faces," she has noted. "It's sensual, it's sexual. At times it's just damned frightening."

Raised in Flint, Michigan, and Scottsdale, Arizona, Bernhard spent eight months farming on a kibbutz in Israel before heading for the comedy-club scene in Los Angeles. She was not an instant success and supported herself by manicuring the fingernails of the rich and famous. ("I dug sand out from under [Dyan Cannon's] big toenail," she later revealed.) But then a few bit parts (in a Cheech and Chong film and in a Muppet movie) got her noticed. When opportunity knocked, she was ready with a script she had cowritten for a stage show called *Without You I'm Nothing,* which showcased all her talents and was turned into a film in 1990. Despite critical acclaim, Bernhard's movie career never took off, but cult notoriety came from her numerous David Letterman appearances, on which she proved to be a formidable foil for the cranky host. One in particular, with her friend Madonna, led to speculation that the two women were lovers. (In 1998 she revealed whe was pregnant, without further explanation.) Bernhard recently returned to the stage with *I'm Still Here . . . Damn It!,* in which she muses on the thought process that goes into naming new perfumes: "Okay, you're in competition with your best friend. You covet everything she has. You're jealous, you're bitter. You even want her husband. You're a back-stabbing bitch: 'Envy,' by Gucci. Yes!" ∎

**"I hated the contrivance of stand-up,"
Bernhard (in London, in 1995) has said.
"I developed a hostile style to get control."**

LEFT: DOUGLAS KIRKLAND/SYGMA; RIGHT: ©SMITH/CAMERA PRESS/RETNA LTD.

"She can make anything funny," said *A League of Their Own* director Penny Marshall of Rosie (in 1993).

She spiked the tired talk show with the chocolate milk of human kindness

Rosie O'DONNELL

THERE'S A CODE ROSIE O'DONNELL USES—"XL"—TO tell her writers she loves a joke but is nixing it, usually because it's "funny but mean." And, as she has said, "I don't want to do mean." That may not sound like a winning formula for an oversaturated talk show market in this XL Age of Springer and Stern. Yet Rosie not only sold her pilot, but created a megahit. Reminiscent of the Mike Douglas and Dinah Shore shows she had loved as a kid, O'Donnell's syndicated program seduced viewers away from trash talk with lightweight celebrity interviews peppered with I'm-a-Regular-Gal-and-You're-My-Hero fawning over the guests. Leaving the movies, where she had been second banana to Meg Ryan *(Sleepless in Seattle)* and Madonna *(A League of Their Own)*, O'Donnell is now the center of a universe where she can brag about her Happy Meal toy collection or belt out classic TV theme songs with the gusto of an Ethel Merman. Better still, her schedule has allowed her to step into the one role that she'd always dreamed of, that of mother—to her adopted kids Parker and Chelsea.

A Long Island, New York, girl who treasured trips to Manhattan, where she would sit high in the third balcony of Radio City Music Hall with her mom (who died when Rosie was 10), she grew up with a love of Broadway soundtracks and the TV shows you could see only when you stayed home sick from school. At 12, she pretended to chat with Johnny Carson while examining her skin in the bathroom mirror. Clearly this was a girl with a need to perform. O'Donnell started out on the stand-up circuit, at first recycling Jerry Seinfeld routines before writing her own. Eventually she landed on Broadway in a revival of *Grease* and played Radio City both with her comedy act and as the ratings-boosting host of the Tony Awards. Couldn't have happened to a nicer person. ■

Watching gobs of TV as a girl, said O'Donnell (in 1993, above, and in 1996), "took the place of parenting because my mom had died and my father was bereft."

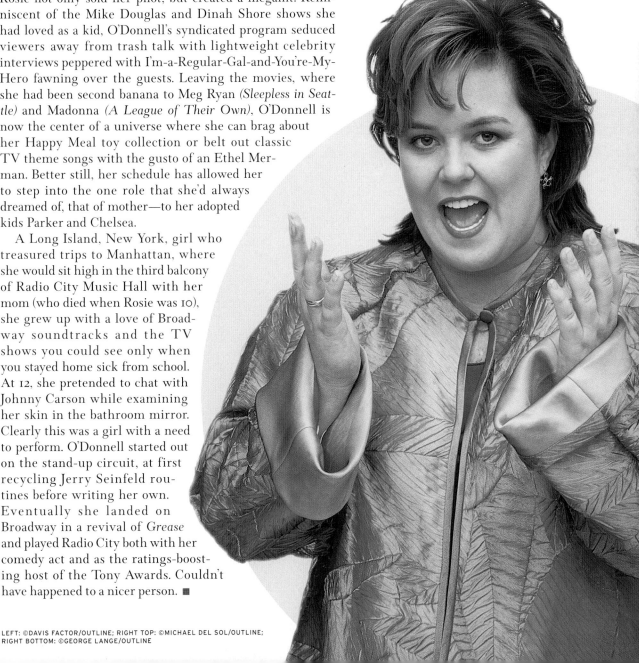

Diane
KEATON

The woman can act, but let us now praise Annie Hall, afloat in her priceless dither

"I always look sober and normal when compared to Keaton," said Woody Allen of his former costar and girlfriend (in 1992). "I turn into the straight man."

Y EAH, WELL, JEEZ, YOU KNOW . . ." It may not be as sexy a line as "Come up and see me sometime," but it worked for Diane Keaton. Inherent in that string of tentative syllables is the message that—her doe-eyed beauty notwithstanding—Keaton is an unassuming gal with nice, normal neuroses woven into her fiber. But is it Keaton talking or Annie Hall—her Oscar-winning title character, she of the baggy khakis, floppy hats and lah-de-dah sighs?

A little of both, really. Born Diane Hall in Orange County, California, she migrated to Manhattan at 19 (taking her mother's maiden name), caught on as an understudy in Broadway's *Hair* and broke through opposite Woody Allen in his 1969 play, *Play It Again, Sam*. She became his muse and lover and the model for Annie, the not-too-ambitious singer and space-cadet cutie in their 1977 film. Al Pacino and Warren Beatty (her costars in *The Godfather* and *Reds*, respectively), also romanced Keaton offscreen. Never married, Keaton adopted a daughter, Dexter, in 1995. Not just a hippy-dippy cartoon, the actress racked up nuanced but little-seen performances in *Shoot the Moon* and *The Good Mother* before returning to comedy in the '90s in films including *Father of the Bride* and *The First Wives Club*.

Like Annie, Keaton swore off Manhattan for Los Angeles, where she ducked behind the camera. Her first feature, *Unstrung Heroes*, was a moving account of a boy and the two eccentric uncles he lived with during his mother's illness. Unlike her flaky alter ego, Keaton took the work seriously and earned critical accolades. But the movie had its Annie-esque quirks: Keaton dislikes the color blue, so no sky appeared on film, and jeans were dyed darker. Okay, well, gosh. Or, as Keaton has said, speaking of her career generally, "Yeah, interesting, the whole thing." ∎

Erma BOMBECK

Hail the harried housewife's defender

T HE WISECRACKING CHAMPION OF THE AMERICAN HOUSEWIFE found absurdity in everything from dirty ovens ("If it won't catch fire today, clean it tomorrow") to divorce ("I'm too old to shop around"). But she never condescended to homemakers, valuing the family stability she herself had lost at 9 when the bank repossessed her childhood home in Dayton—along with all the furniture—after her crane-operator father died of a stroke. She coped by taking a comic view of life, writing her first humor column for the school paper at 13. At an after-school job for the *Dayton Herald*, she met *Dayton Journal* copy clerk Bill Bombeck and married him after graduating from the University of Dayton. Determined to give their three children the attention her factory worker mother had been unable to provide, Bombeck dropped out of newspapering for 12 years. And even after she began writing her column, *At Wit's End*, for $3 a week, her family came first. Son Andrew once remarked, "Mom never missed dinner because of a deadline." She later honed her suburban one-liners in bestsellers such as *The Grass Is Always Greener over the Septic Tank*. Although she expressed impatience with dour feminist militants, she stumped tirelessly for the ERA in the 1970s. In 1992, Bombeck's life began to unravel on a far deeper level than the day-to-day trials she lampooned, starting with a mastectomy that, her husband said, left her "deeply shaken." Soon after, her kidneys began to fail (she had been diagnosed with polycystic kidney disease at 20). To encourage her sons, who had inherited the condition ("the gift," she said sardonically, "that keeps on giving"), Bombeck made light of the situation. Until her death, at 69, from complications following a kidney transplant, she would scold distressed readers: "Never feel sorry for a humorist." ∎

"I am lucky," says Loren (vamping in 1955). "I had a very beautiful mother."

Venus Rising

THIS PANTHEON OF PULCHRITUDE LIT UP OUR MOVIE SCREENS AND DAYDREAMS

Sophia Loren

Who says our favorite imported Neapolitan dish was pizza?

TECHETTO," THEY CALLED HER AS A PRETEEN, "THE STICK." SOFIA SCICOLONE WAS A WAIF OF A girl, with little to hint at the voluptuous beauty that would transcend language and make her a star on both sides of the Atlantic. Raised by her mother in the postwar slums of Naples, she was skinny but not entirely unpleasant to look at—all she needed was some filling out. "Everything you see," she once said, "I owe to spaghetti." At age 15 she entered a beauty contest, and one of the judges suggested she might have a future in film. He was the producer Carlo Ponti, and six years later the two would marry. Ponti helped her find the right director, Vittorio De Sica, who became a father figure to the fatherless young star and linked her with the perfect leading man. Working with Marcello Mastroianni elevated La Loren to international sex-symbol status in the '60s. He was the howling wolf to her teasing vixen in *Yesterday, Today and Tomorrow* and *Marriage Italian-Style* (and, in a 1994 encore, in *Prêt-à-Porter*, in which the pair reprised their roles as ardent lovers who, this time, fell asleep before the good part). But it was a 1961 role, in which Loren was cast against type, that won her an Oscar. In *Two Women*, based on an Alberto Moravia novel, she played the mother who is raped while trying to protect her daughter. Originally picked by De Sica to play the more glamorous child, Loren was later recast in the older part, proving herself as an actress and saying something important about herself. She and Ponti have remained together for over 30 years, as she has dedicated herself to raising their two sons. She doesn't lie about her age (63) and notes that if she were beginning her career now, she couldn't conduct herself like today's stars. "Sharon Stone talks about sex as if she were talking about a bowl of spaghetti or a pizza," Loren once observed. "These things are private; you need a bit of discretion." ■

Still stunning, Loren has insisted that she never has had cosmetic surgery and that she cuts and dyes her own hair.

Garbo (in 1931) valued independence since she was a young girl and had to leave school to care for her sick father.

Greta Garbo

She achieved great fame, only to run from it

REMARKABLY, GRETA GARBO ENTERED HOLLYWOOD MOVIES NOT ON THE strength of her talent and ethereal beauty but as part of a package deal Louis B. Mayer had cut in order to sign her countryman, Swedish director Mauritz Stiller. Garbo, he felt, was too fat. But audiences of the 1920s adored her in a string of silents; and, in 1930, two years into the talkie revolution, ads for *Anna Christie* were finally able to promise, "Garbo Talks!" Indeed, 34 minutes after the opening credits, her lilting, accented purr debuted: "Gimme a viskey with chincher ale on the side, and don't be stingy, baby."

Inner life was overriding to Garbo, and she felt no obligation to explain herself. She had a hot affair with an early costar, John Gilbert, but on their wedding day, Garbo simply did not show up. After her last film, *Two-Faced Women*, made when she was 36, Garbo retired and lived a life so notoriously cloistered that her cherished privacy rivaled her acting achievements as what she would be remembered for. She would book two seats on a plane to sit by herself, walk incognito through New York City or else employ the alias "Harriet Brown." When she died in 1990, at 84, the hospital released no details of her passing. In her last years she chided even close friends, "Don't ever ask me about the movies, especially why I left them." The answer was not only a mystery, it was a tragedy. ∎

Marlene Dietrich

Manipulating androgyny gave her universal appeal

ER HUSBAND, CZECH CASTING DIRECTOR RUDOLF SIEBER, ONCE SAID THAT TWO PEOPLE lived in his wife's body: "one, strong like a man; the other, soft like a woman." Marlene Dietrich was film's first gender-bender. She wore a tuxedo to marvelous erotic effect in *The Blue Angel* (1930), kissed a woman in *Morocco* (also 1930) and had numerous offscreen lovers (whose letters she shared with Sieber), including both John Wayne and Edith Piaf. "In Europe," said Dietrich, a German expatriate, "we make love with anyone we find attractive."

Berlin-born Maria Magdalene Dietrich might have been a violinist had she not injured her hand at age 18. Instead she took up acting and won stage roles in Germany. As Dietrich grew famous, she and Sieber separated but never divorced. (He would later become a chicken farmer in California.) Film director Josef von Sternberg saw Dietrich in a play and cast her as the sultry Lola-Lola in *The Blue Angel*. Their long partnership established her femme fatale credentials. In 1937, Adolf Hitler asked her to name her price to come back to Germany. Dietrich, who had helped Jewish friends escape, refused. Her films were then banned in her homeland. Granted U.S. citizenship, she entertained Allied troops, singing and playing a musical saw. When she could no longer hide her advancing age in close-ups, she became a cabaret star, sharing bills with the Beatles. Later she dropped out of sight altogether. Unlike rival Greta Garbo, who wanted to undo her celebrity, Dietrich wanted to preserve it and be remembered as she was. Only a few people, including her four grandsons, who loved her apple strudel, saw her at home. In 1992, at 90, she died in the Paris apartment she hadn't left for five years. At her request, Dietrich was buried in Germany, where mourners declared, "The Blue Angel does not die." ∎

Hearing that Madonna might remake *Blue Angel*, Dietrich (in a 1930s publicity still) cried, "Oh, puh-leeze!"

Ava Gardner

Her siren song lured leading men but never led to lasting love

A GREEN-EYED TIGRESS BILLED BY A MOVIE PUBLICIST AS "THE WORLD'S MOST BEAU-tiful animal," Ava Gardner never really escaped the prison of her pulchritude. Daughter of a sharecropper and a boardinghouse landlady, she was going to become a secretary until a Hollywood flunky spied her picture in her brother-in-law's New York City photo studio and arranged for a screen test. It was silent because of her thick North Carolina accent, but MGM wired back, "She can't act, she didn't talk, she's sensational. Get her out here." Gardner started slowly but made her name after WW II in *The Killers*, *Mogambo* (her only Oscar nomination) and the sadly prophetic *The Barefoot Contessa*, as a Spanish dancer transformed into a screen goddess who couldn't find personal happiness. Her brief marriages, to Mickey Rooney (a press agent tagged along on their honeymoon), Frank Sinatra (he reportedly tried suicide to show his love) and bandleader Artie Shaw (he had her psychoanalyzed) led Gardner to say she should have married a garage mechanic back home. Exiling herself to Europe in the late 1950s, she dallied with Spanish matadors but never found her soulmate or self-respect, once remarking before her death of pneumonia, at 67, in 1990, "I was never really an actress. None of us kids who came from MGM were. We were just good to look at." ∎

Gardner (in the 1940s) said she would have traded her career for "one good man I could love and marry and cook for and make a home for, who would stick around for the rest of my life."

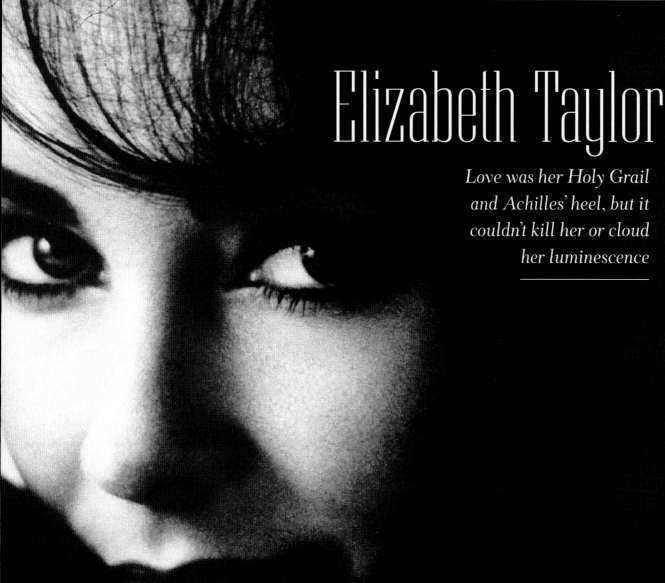

Elizabeth Taylor

*Love was her Holy Grail
and Achilles' heel, but it
couldn't kill her or cloud
her luminescence*

TABLOID WRITERS LICKED THEIR CHOPS, CHRONICLING A LIFE MARKED BY calamity, including seven divorces. But from her own 66-year world view through those most observed—and wryly observant—violet eyes, Taylor sees a life filled with love: the love of seven men, four children and many grandchildren, friends and fans. A screen presence from age 10, she made a seamless transition from ingenue of the 1940s in *National Velvet* to lustrous leading lady in *Giant*, picked up five Oscar nominations, winning for *Butterfield 8* and *Who's Afraid of Virginia Woolf.* Currently retired (except for a plum role like Wilma's mother in *The Flintstones)*, she expresses her love philanthropically. As an AIDS activist, Taylor was well-ahead of Hollywood's red-ribbon-wearing pack, raising money and understanding after her old pal and *Giant* costar Rock Hudson died from the disease in 1985. Her personal life, meanwhile, was a roller coaster. Whether she was cutting in on the Debbie Reynolds-Eddie Fisher marriage as if it were a dance, trysting with Richard Burton on the lavish playground set of *Cleopatra* or picking up her last husband, construction worker Larry Fortensky, at the Betty Ford Center, she was a one-woman survival course. Aside from all the heartbreak, she has simultaneously pulled through a string of near-fatal illnesses, from pill addiction to pneumonia and a brain tumor, with resilience and endearing good humor. As a doctor woke her from her last operation, she caught sight of his wedding ring. "Mmm," cooed Taylor, "I've had a lot of those." ∎

The celeb's celeb, Taylor (in 1958) has bonded with Michael Jackson over their public childhoods and elicits starstruck responses from even the super-cool. "She takes my breath away," says Madonna.

Can Pfeiffer (in 1998) protect herself? Attests Cher: "It's not possible to mess with her and come out on top."

Michelle Pfeiffer

They knew right away she was The Bombshell

A CALIFORNIA SURFER GIRL WITH GRACE KELLY-LIKE COOL, MICHELLE PFEIFFER figured that life had miscast her as a supermarket checkout clerk the day a customer blamed her for the lousy produce. So at 19 she tried modeling, became Miss Orange County and wound up in a TV spinoff of *Animal House*—she played the bit role billed simply as The Bombshell. That led to *Grease 2*, a flop sequel, but then she bugged Brian dePalma until he put her in *Scarface* (opposite Al Pacino). With just a few acting lessons along the way, Pfeiffer ranged with surprising ease from a songstress in *The Fabulous Baker Boys* to the whip-cracking Catwoman in *Batman Returns* and a mysterious countess in *The Age of Innocence*. Three Oscar nominations fell into her lap, as did two choice husbands: Peter (*thirtysomething*) Horton, for seven years, followed, since 1993, by David Kelley, the hot TV producer-writer of *Picket Fences* and *Ally McBeal*. Already having adopted a daughter, she and Kelley then had a son, but what worried Pfeiffer was the cinemalogical clock. At 41 she formed a production company and acquired the Oprah's Book Club sensation *The Deep End of the Ocean*. "Look at Jessica [Lange] and Meryl [Streep] and Catherine Deneuve," she says hopefully. "Maybe I have a few years out there that I didn't think I had." ■

Isabella Rossellini

Her lineage is a gift she shares with the camera

In the 1990s she lost Lancôme and love David Lynch but adopted a son, Roberto, to go along with daughter Elettra.

WHEN YOU HAVE FAMOUS PARENTS, everybody in the world has an idea of who they are," says actress-model Isabella Rossellini, 46. And, by extension, who you are. Like her mother, Ingrid Bergman, she got pregnant by another man (model Jonathan Wiedemann) while married—to Martin Scorsese, a director like her father, Roberto Rossellini. But in her day, infidelity didn't cause a global scandal. She then wed Wiedemann, but after two years wound up with David Lynch, her director in *Blue Velvet*. Writers wondered if she took up with directors in search of a father figure and if her acting could match Bergman's. She's glorious to look at, like Mom, and speaks in the warm, Mediterranean tones of Dad, but as she wrote in *Some of Me*, her charming if obfuscating memoir, Rossellini is more than celebrated genes. ■

Iman

*Her name means
priest, and for 20 years
she has been the high
priestess of modeling*

**Iman (at work in
1995) used her
fame to make a
BBC film about
the 1992 civil war
and famine in her
homeland, and
later she implored
the U.S. Senate to
send aid.**

EVERY TIME I'M ON
a runway, I deliber-
ately think of Somalia,
and I try to take the people
watching me to where I am in my
head." Few people have been where
Iman has. Who of her compatriots has
known the couture scene from the inside?
And who of her fellow *fashionistas* can imagine growing up in Mogadishu? Her parents, a
diplomat and a gynecologist, were wealthy and
liberated, but Iman saw poverty and the oppressive
misogyny of the culture. She began modeling after photographer Peter Beard spotted her at the University of
Nairobi. (Beard took credit for her success, though the
Iman of his fanciful recollection is a goatherd, not a student.) But it is her timeless beauty—those cheekbones!
that neck!—that got her all those gigs once consigned to
blue-eyed blondes. Now she is into acting and entrepre-
neurship, selling cosmetics for women of color. With a
daughter from an earlier marriage to basketball player
Spencer Haywood, she lives with rocker husband David
Bowie. "I've gotten this far," she says unfazed by turning
43. "The next 40 will be a piece of cake." ■

Catherine Deneuve

A model of Paris chic, she is France—literally

SHE PLAYED PORCELAIN BEAUTIES WITH SECRET LIVES: THE BOURGEOIS DOCTOR'S WIFE OF *Belle de Jour*, working afternoons in a Paris brothel; *Repulsion*'s sexually repressed manicurist, lapsing into razor-wielding madness. Deneuve, too, is a woman of contradiction. "It's not in my nature to be looked at," the amber-eyed actress once confessed, though as Brigitte Bardot's replacement as the model for Marianne (an Uncle Sam-like symbol of the Republic), her image is emblazoned on French stamps. She has been called the most beautiful woman in the world and also an ice queen. "In France," Annie Cohen-Solal, cultural counselor at the French Embassy in New York City, once explained, "the height of sophistication has to be minimal. It's a very specific, delicate level that you very seldom reach—and that's where she is."

The onetime Catholic school girl, daughter of Parisian actors, defied convention by moving in at 17 with director Roger Vadim, then bearing his son and refusing to marry him. She was briefly wed to swinging '60s photographer David Bailey (the bride wore black Yves St. Laurent) and later had a daughter by Marcello Mastroianni. Now a grandmother, Deneuve, 54, still makes movies (she won an Oscar nomination for 1992's *Indochine*), goes salsa dancing (with daughter Chiara and her boyfriend) and gardens. "I don't try to charm," she has said. "I have quite strong and straight relations with people. In film it's different. In films you are a character and woman—much more woman than me." Mystery, thy name is Deneuve. ■

"Managing Catherine [in *Belle de Jour*, 1967]," said ex-husband Bailey, "was like trying to manage a Maserati when you're used to a Ford."

Gandhi (campaigning in a 1978 election) had been voted out of India's presidency in favor of an opposition leader she'd once jailed.

movers & SHAPERS

INDIRA GANDHI

Vowing to be 'not merely a daughter,' she succeeded only too well

RAISED IN A HOME THAT DOUBLED AS HEADQUARTERS FOR THE INDIAN INDEPENDENCE movement, a very young Indira Gandhi invented highly politicized childhood games, including playacting Joan of Arc. Martyrdom was almost taken for granted as she often watched her parents, Jawaharlal and Kamala Nehru, being arrested and jailed. Schooled in India and at Oxford, she too was imprisoned with her husband, newspaperman Feroze Gandhi (no relation to Mohandas); they later had two sons and separated. When the country threw off British rule in 1947, her father became the first prime minister, and she took the post in 1966. "In politics one has to work doubly hard to show one is not merely a daughter but a person in her own right," Gandhi once noted of her problems in leading the world's most populous democracy. She may have inherited power, but with it, a country having warred with neighboring Pakistan and much of its more than 500 million people living in poverty.

While Gandhi had many successes in office—helping to establish an independent Bangladesh and bringing India into the space race—excesses of ego betrayed her. Accused of election abuses, she used vestigial British laws to declare a state of emergency, throwing opposition leaders in jail and censoring the media. In 1977 she was voted out, and faced charges of corruption. But her legal battles only brought her more admiration, and she was returned to power three years later. In 1984, shortly after she ordered government troops to quell a separatist Sikh rebellion in Punjab, Gandhi was murdered, at age 66, by her Sikh bodyguards. Her son Rajiv succeeded her, both as prime minister and as the target of political violence: He was assassinated during a reelection campaign. A mother had left her son the only legacy she knew. ■

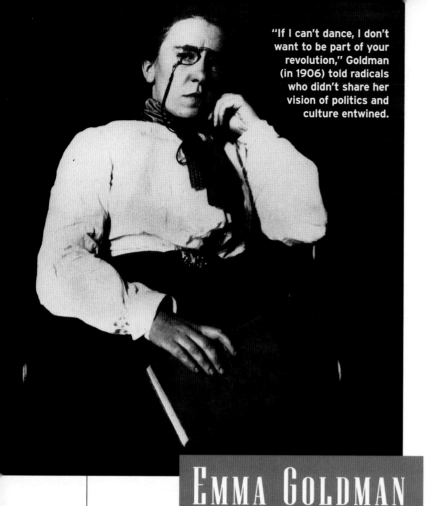

"If I can't dance, I don't want to be part of your revolution," Goldman (in 1906) told radicals who didn't share her vision of politics and culture entwined.

EMMA GOLDMAN

She fought for unfettered freedom

ONCE BRANDED BY J. EDGAR HOOVER AS "THE most dangerous woman in America," Emma Goldman had been spurred to radicalism by the inhumane treatment she received as a Russian immigrant in a Rochester, New York, sweatshop. At age 20, she left her American husband and eventually moved to New York City with, she said, "five dollars and a small handbag," to pursue her belief in feminism and utopian anarchy. There she lived with lover Alexander Berkman, who plotted to bump off steel mogul Henry Clay Frick during an 1892 strike.

Frick survived the shooting. Goldman, who had actually opposed the plot, took to the lecture circuit to demand food relief for the unemployed and free speech for all. An early advocate of birth control (Margaret Sanger was too mainstream for her), Red Emma thought marriage enslaved women. But she herself was a slave to her passion for longtime lover Dr. Ben Reitman, who humiliated her by using her lectures on free love as opportunities to pick up women. Goldman was jailed for nearly two years for WWI draft protests and, in 1919, deported to Russia (giving rise to her 1923 screed, *My Disillusionment in Russia*). When she was allowed to return for a visit in 1934, six years before her death, at 70, thousands turned out to hear the still-fiery radical speak. ∎

"There have been many tragedies," King (at a 1963 rally in Birmingham) said in 1998, ". . . but I don't look at them as painful."

CORETTA SCOTT KING

With grace and grit, she keeps striving to achieve her husband's dream

THE SEEDS OF HER LIFELONG STRUGGLE AGAINST racism were sown in her Alabama childhood, when a bus carrying white youngsters passed her each day on the five-mile hike to her segregated one-room schoolhouse. Later her mother, a farmer's wife with a fourth-grade education, struck back by renting a bus so that Coretta Scott and the other rural black students could travel the 10 miles to high school. This example of unyielding determination would serve the daughter well when she married preacher Martin Luther King Jr. in 1953, shortly after they had met in Boston, where she attended the New England Conservatory of Music, hoping to become a singer. Instead, the couple raised their voices for freedom. Coretta remained focused through the jailings and the bombings, coolly fielding the barrage of hate calls while raising four children. When King was assassinated in Memphis, in 1968, the widow, 40, led a protest march there four days later. She has continued to speak out for justice as the founder of the Martin Luther King Jr. Center for Nonviolent Social Change, which sponsors voter registration, literacy and other programs. "His vibrant legacy of nonviolent social change," she once wrote, "will continue to inspire millions." ∎

A compelling mix of
intellect and glamor
made Steinem (at
Ms. in 1972) what
the press dubbed
"the thinking man's
Jean Shrimpton."

GLORIA STEINEM

Ever the activist, she gave feminism a fresh face and a new energy

A WOMAN NEEDS A MAN LIKE A FISH NEEDS A BICYCLE." THAT PROVOCATIVE 1970s CHAL-
lenge turned up the heat of the women's rights movement from simmer to rolling
boil. In the process, the quip's author—journalist Gloria Steinem—became American feminism's most persuasive and controversial public icon. Her profile was only
enhanced, because she herself seemed a fish out of water. Susan Faludi, the second-generation
feminist and author, told the *Los Angeles Times* regarding Steinem's avoidance of stereotypes,
"She's attractive, has a personal life. She's funny, which makes her a constant irritation to those
who would dismiss feminism as a gathering of sour-faced, bonneted suffragettes."

Raised in Toledo, Ohio, Steinem tended to her mentally ill, divorced mother, Ruth, before
heading for college. After graduating magna cum laude from Smith College, she became an
enterprising reporter, contributing to magazines such as *Glamour* and *New York*. In 1963 she
went undercover as a Playboy Bunny to detail what she saw as the exploitation of the women
who worked as briefly-clad waitresses in Hugh Hefner's nightclubs. Steinem went on to be a co-
founder of *Ms.* magazine, in 1971, and served as its committed editor for 16 years, publicizing
women's travails and triumphs, from workplace issues to the inflammatory debate over reproductive rights. She battled for causes ranging from Native American rights to the plight of
farm workers, and became a leader of the National Organization of Women. "I once thought I
would do this for two or three years," she said of her activism, "and then go home to my real life.
But that was just a symptom of the movement's tone at the time."

Her personal life sometimes belied the public stance. The never-mar-
ried Steinem, who had an abortion at 22, fell for the wrong guy more than
once. She had a three-year relationship with publishing scion Mort Zuck-
erman that ended in 1987. And she often forgot to take care of Gloria. In her
1992 book, *Revolution from Within*, she admitted that "I, too, was more
aware of other people's feelings than my own." But she remains, as she once
said, "a congenital optimist," and the 64-year-old breast cancer survivor
isn't ready to put on a sour face and bonnet. "A friend and I used to joke that
we were going to be pioneer dirty old ladies," she quipped to PEOPLE in
1995, "on bar stools, in too-tight skirts, giving Boy Scouts money for sex." ∎

Battling stereo-
types with
humor, Steinem
(at a 1996 NOW
rally) remarked
that she'd never
burned her bra
or had even seen
one singed.

A frontline trooper,
Steinem was arrested
during a 1984
apartheid protest
outside the South
African embassy in
Washington.

Aquino's signature yellow outfits became a symbol of Philippine democracy.

CORAZON AQUINO

Taking up her slain husband's cause, she led a ballot-box revolution

CORAZON AQUINO WAS IN BOSTON WHEN her husband was killed upon his return to Manila in 1983. She could have stayed in America with her five boys. Instead, she threw herself back into the hell that was the Philippines under Ferdinand Marcos and took up Benigno Aquino Jr.'s cause to oust the dictator. "It was never my intention," she said, "to seek the presidency. But sometimes life does not proceed as you expected it to." Indeed it did not for Marcos—whom Aquino blamed for her husband's murder. He was voted out in favor of this homemaker and political novice.

One of eight children born to a sugar baron, she married Benigno a year before he became mayor of a Philippine city. For 28 years she was a politician's wife, until widowhood gave her a new calling. "The only thing I can really offer the Filipino people," Aquino said, "is my sincerity." That was enough in a country ready for democracy after 20 years of martial law. She provided a new constitution and an independent supreme court, and lifted press censorship. But most of the nation still suffered dire poverty; the military was divided, and much of the government was still corrupt. Aquino withstood several coup attempts and lasted until the elections of 1992, when she chose not to run. In the 1985 campaign, so many hopes had been pinned on Aquino that many wished her to be "mother of the nation." But she was clear in her purpose: "I will remain a mother to my children, but I intend to be chief executive of this nation." ■

MARGARET THATCHER

Preaching no-pain-no-gain, a grocer's daughter shook up a shopworn economy

SHE REACHED 10 DOWNING STREET BY GRIT, GOOD timing and a fierce belief in self-reliance, instilled by her adored shopkeeper father, a methodic Methodist who became town mayor. "The advantage of this childhood," wrote author John Mortimer, "was that it gave the budding Conservative the strength to impose the values of the corner shop on the politics of a nation. The disadvantage was that it made her quite unable to understand, or even tolerate, those whose aims, ideals and ambitions were entirely different."

Bright and outgoing, Margaret Roberts attended Oxford on scholarship, then steadily ascended in Conservative party ranks. In 1951 she married Denis Thatcher—confident businessman, golfer and staunch supporter ("I chose the right husband"). Though she had been excluded from Oxford's all-male debating society, Thatcher riveted the House of Commons as an orator following her election to Parliament in 1959. Becoming Britain's first female prime minister, in 1979, she used feminine wiles and ignored feminist issues. Her staunch anticommunism earned her the nickname "Iron Lady" and the admiration of President Reagan (though she reportedly informed him that, as a former chemist, she knew his beloved Star Wars defense system wouldn't work). "Being conservative," she once wrote, "is never merely a matter of income, but a whole way of life, a will to take responsibility for oneself." Exerting her own inexorable will, she broke the grip of the trade unions, curbed inflation, privatized industry and demolished the welfare state. On the dark side, unemployment zoomed and class resentments boiled over in the punk rebellion. In 1990 her support of an unpopular poll tax forced Thatcher to resign. If her legacy is mixed, her achievements are indisputable. ∎

"I like people who will not compromise one inch," said Thatcher (addressing Conservative party delegates in 1978). "I cannot stand wishy-washy men."

"Even more important than being first," said O'Connor (in 1994, a year after Ruth Bader Ginsberg joined her), "is not being the last."

"I think to be free is to be able to do what you think is right," said Suu Kyi (at home in Rangoon in 1995). "In that sense I felt very free, even under house arrest."

SANDRA DAY O'CONNOR

Justice was served as she broke a 191-year barrier

S ANDRA DAY DEVELOPED A DISTASTE FOR LONG BUS RIDES THE year she had to rise at dawn to attend a school 32 miles from her family's New Mexico ranch. And she got firsthand exposure to discrimination when, after graduating third in her class at Stanford law, "the only job offer I received was as a legal secretary." Years later those memories shaped her opinion that busing was no solution to school segregation, and that it was important not to make "inaccurate assumptions about the proper roles of men and women."

The scion of a cattle family, she married law classmate John Jay O'Connor, a military man who relocated the newlyweds to Germany. After three years the couple settled in Arizona, and O'Connor went into private practice as a litigator, taking off four years to begin raising their three sons. Shortly after her return to the job force, in the attorney general's office, she was chosen to serve out a state senate term. After two terms she ran for a superior court judgeship and was later appointed to an appeals court, the field from which she was plucked by President Reagan in 1981 to be his Supreme Court nominee. Neither being a woman nor a moderate conservative made O'Connor's votes predictable (yes, on upholding *Roe v. Wade*; no, on state funding for abortion). As the first woman judge in the high court's 191-year history, O'Connor made some small adjustments herself. After a boozy Washington Redskins running back, John Riggins, advised her at a party, "Come on, Sandy baby, loosen up," O'Connor, 68, started an exercise class for the court's female staffers, with T-shirts that read, "Loosen up with the Supremes." ■

DAW AUNG SAN SUU KYI

While held by force at home alone, she inspired a fight for Burmese democracy

MOST OF THE WORLD HAD NEVER HEARD OF DAW Aung San Suu Kyi until her government placed her under house arrest in 1989. Cut off from her family and the press, and unable to phone out or post a letter, she still drew world attention to the oppression of Burmese military rule. Word of her persecution leaked out, and, even while captive in her home, she was awarded the 1991 Nobel Peace Prize.

She is the daughter of a man she never knew but knew about: General Aung San, who had helped win Burma's independence from Britain and was assassinated by right-wing extremists in 1947, when Suu Kyi was 2. In 1962, two years after she left to study economics in India and England, Burma fell to a military coup. In the ensuing decades she would marry a British scholar, Michael Aris, and raise two sons; she had little interest in politics. But when she returned in 1988 to nurse her dying mother, Suu Kyi saw students pouring into the streets, demonstrating against the government, and an army shooting them down by the hundreds. "As my father's daughter," she said, "I felt I had a duty to get involved." Later that year, Suu Kyi helped form the National League of Democracy. In 1989 she was arrested, separated for six years from her husband and teenage boys, who had remained in England. Today, still living alone in Burma (renamed Myanmar), she has tirelessly attempted negotiation with the military leaders, who won't acknowledge elections that voted her NLD Party into power in 1990. Suu Kyi won the hearts of her people and the admiration of millions, but she dreams of fulfilling the promise of her given name, which means "a bright collection of strange victories." ■

Ride (in Houston, '83) called her debut flight "the most fun I'll ever have in my life."

"Sometimes I just say that Mankiller is my name, that I earned it, and I let 'em wonder," remarked the ex-chief of the Cherokee Nation (in 1988).

SALLY RIDE

Our first woman astronaut stressed 'astronaut'

BEING FIRST WAS FAMILIAR TO SALLY RIDE. SHE WAS OFTEN picked first—even before the boys—when the kids in her Los Angeles suburb chose up teams for sports. Years later, while finishing her Ph.D. in physics at Stanford, she noticed an ad in the school paper: NASA wanted scientists for its astronaut program. On a whim she applied. From 8,000 hopefuls, NASA chose 35 candidates—six of them women. Ride was chosen for a 1983 *Challenger* shuttle mission that made her the first American female in space. She downplayed the pioneer aspect, saying, "I did not come to NASA to make history," and adding it was achievement enough to join the elite club of 57 other Americans who had flown in space. Besides, the Russians had sent up a woman 20 years earlier, and for all the accolades there was still chauvinism: Johnny Carson joked that Ride was holding up the launch looking for a purse to match her space shoes. She flew a second shuttle mission the next year, and was scheduled for a third when the *Challenger* exploded after launch in 1986. Later, Ride was assigned to a team investigating the disaster. Now 47 and back at Stanford in a security-and-arms-control think tank, she is occasionally reminded of her place in history: "When an 8-year-old girl asks me what to do to become an astronaut, I like that." ■

WILMA MANKILLER

She advanced her people's cause by blending modern ways with native culture

WHEN THE FEDERAL GOVERNMENT FORCED HER Cherokee family to move from Oklahoma to San Francisco, where jobs were assumed to be more plentiful, Wilma Pearl, 10, didn't know how to use a phone or ride a bike. Her father, a union organizer, helped her adjust to the new culture while maintaining her identity. Years later the women's movement gave the then-unhappily-married housewife a voice. Finally, the 1969 occupation of Alcatraz Island by young Indians trying to bring attention to Native American issues put it all into focus. Divorcing her husband, Pearl resumed her Cherokee name, Mankiller (a traditional military title similar to captain) and returned to Oklahoma with her two daughters. In 1985 she was elected the first female chief of a major Indian tribe. Neither a near-fatal car crash nor a kidney transplant deterred her from implementing her ambitious programs, like job training, college scholarships, housing and health clinics. Lymphoma forced her to step down, at 50. "Movies always seem to show Indian women washing clothes at the creek and men with a tomahawk," says Mankiller (still politically active and happily remarried). "We're rarely depicted as real people ... trying to hang on to our culture." ∎

MARIE CURIE

The widowed mom refused to fold

THE WORK WAS BACKBREAKING: LONG days spent stirring a cauldron of uranium ore, with an iron rod the size of her arm, as she and her husband, Pierre, sought to isolate the material's radioactive components. But the payoff was astounding. With the discovery of the elements polonium and then radium, Marie Curie jump-started the study of radioactivity (she even coined the term) and became the first person ever to win two Nobel Prizes, one for Physics and one for Chemistry. "It was in this miserable old shed," she later wrote, "that the best and happiest years of our life were spent, entirely consecrated to work."

For Curie, there was no higher purpose. Born in Warsaw, in 1867—the youngest of five children of a school official—Marie found her gift for science blocked by her homeland's ban on women's attending universities. For six years she toiled as a governess for a Polish family, until she could afford to move to Paris, in 1891, to study at the Sorbonne. There she subsisted on bread and tea—and the inspiration of research in a collaboration of equals with Pierre, a physics professor whom she met in Paris and married in 1895. But in 1906, Pierre was killed by a horse-drawn carriage, leaving her to raise two young daughters alone. The French government offered Marie a pension, but she refused it, insisting, "Whatever happens . . . one must work just the same." She took over Pierre's teaching job at the Sorbonne (becoming the first woman professor in the school's then-650-year history) and used her research with radium to develop portable X-ray machines to examine wounded soldiers in World War I, even driving to the front when necessary to make repairs.

Curie's success didn't sit well with everyone. The chauvinistic French Academy of Sciences refused her membership, and in 1910 the conservative French press tried to smear her reputation by printing intimate letters she'd written to her lover, a married scientist. But Curie, who died in 1934 from leukemia brought on by long exposure to radiation, maintained her dignity. "There is nothing in my acts," she once wrote, "which obliges me to feel diminished." ∎

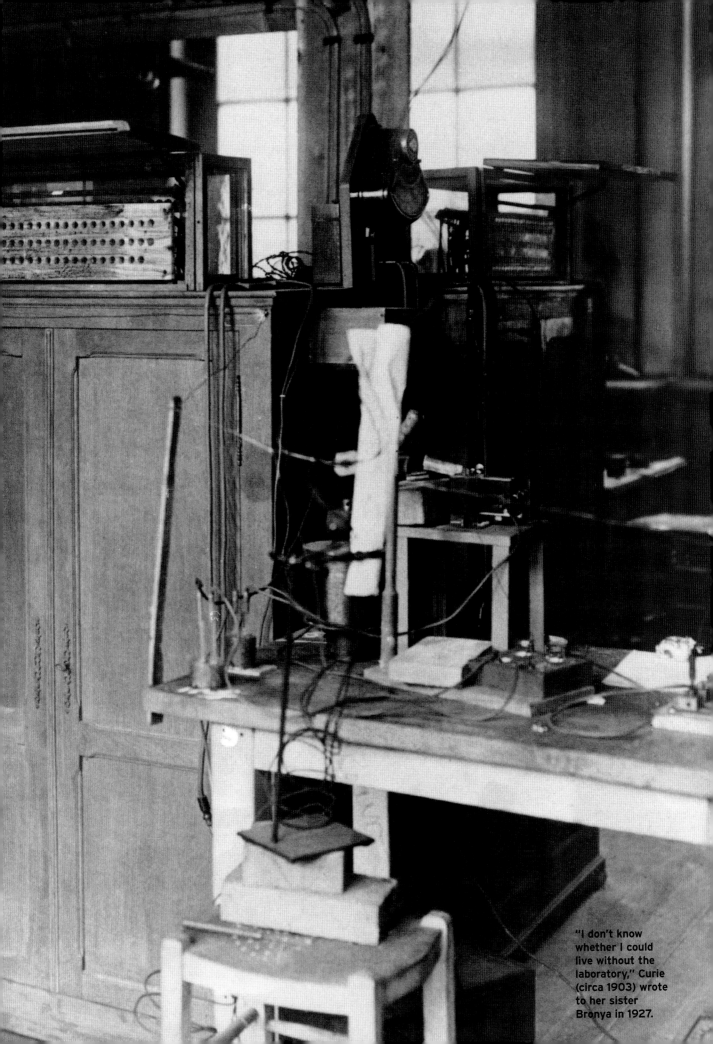

"I don't know whether I could live without the laboratory," Curie (circa 1903) wrote to her sister Bronya in 1927.

Margaret Mead

Energetic to a fault, she saw the universal in the exotic

A T THE AGE OF 8, SHE WAS ASSIGNED TO OBSERVE AND RECORD HER younger sister's speech patterns. "My family," wrote Mead of her sociologist mother and professor father, "deeply disapproved of any school that kept children chained to their desks." Educated at home by her grandmother, a teacher, Mead recalled, "I learned to observe the world around me and to note what I saw." It was ideal preparation for a life of fieldwork in the budding science of anthropology, which she studied with Franz Boas, its founder, at Barnard College. Mead's belief that the study of other cultures could "add immeasurably to our knowledge of who we ourselves are" was seconded in 1928 by the American public—which made *Coming of Age in Samoa*, her absorbing study of adolescent girls, a bestseller and anointed Mead, at 26, a celebrity.

She was delighted. Just as she had enjoyed being the family confidante growing up, so was she eager to share secrets of the primitive peoples she studied. Adventurous in love as in life, she married three times (third husband Gregory Bateson confessed, "I couldn't keep up with her") and carried on a long-term affair with Columbia mentor Ruth Benedict. Mead's daughter chalked up her mother's complex entanglements to "her greed for more and richer experience." But it was probably true, as brother-in-law Leo Rosten remarked, that "she'd rather exchange ideas than kisses." As curator of ethnology at New York City's American Museum of Natural History, Mead relished training the next generation and was an outspoken feminist like her suffragist mother. After she died of cancer, at 76, some debunked her early methods. No one denied Mead had shown it was indeed a small world. ∎

This trail of ancient footprints, preserved in volcanic rock in Tanzania, prompted Leakey to light a cigar and say, in 1978, "Now this really is something to put on the mantelpiece."

"She was such a busybody, she'd run everybody's lives, but they loved it," said former student Ken Heyman of Mead (in Bali, 1938).

MARY LEAKEY

Tracking the origins of the human race, she left footprints that will be hard to fill

T WAS A CASE OF NATURE PLUS NURTURE. SHE WAS A descendant of a British prehistorian who recognized the significance of Stone Age implements as early as 1797. Her own passion grew during jaunts through Europe, where her landscape-painter father introduced her to Cro-Magnon cave art. Back home in London, Mary Nicol was restless in the classroom. Expelled twice, she remarked, "I had never passed a single school exam and clearly never would." A talented artist like her father, she began doing drawings for archaeological digs. She soon met the renowned—and married—Louis Leakey. Their affair eventually cost him his professorship at Cambridge. At 22, she went off with him to Africa, and they married a year later, after his 1936 divorce.

For years she toiled in the shadow of her flamboyant husband, who often took credit for her painstaking work (the two finally separated, after three children). But Mary's 1959 discovery of an early hominid nicknamed "nutcracker man" (for his huge teeth), near the Olduvai Gorge, put her in the spotlight. One expert called it the start of "the truly scientific study of the evolution of man." Her reputation was further enhanced in 1978, when she spied footprints on the Serengeti Plain that proved early humans had walked upright 3.6 million years before. Five years later, failing eyesight caused her to retire to her home in Nairobi. ("Given the chance," she allowed, "I'd rather be in a tent than a house.") Leakey spent her last years before she died, at 83, in 1996, enjoying the African sunsets on the porch while sipping her favorite single-malt Scotch. ▪

DIAN FOSSEY

The naturalist's fierce devotion to her gorillas spurred her isolation and demise

EVEN IN HER YOUTH THE GAWKY SIX-FOOTER, whose bluster masked a disposition as gentle as that of her beloved mountain gorillas, was passionately protective of animals and spent hours of leisure time at the local stable. As an occupational therapist working with disabled children at a Kentucky hospital, after graduating from San Jose State in 1954, the California girl amused her charges by luring squirrels from the woods to be fed. In 1963, Dian Fossey fulfilled a childhood dream of going on safari. ("Africa meant freedom to me, adventure, lack of restraint," she once said.) There she met anthropologist Louis Leakey; three years later, thinking an amateur might be more patient, he engaged the enthusiastic tourist to study gorillas. Her genteel mother said, "I forbid it!" (and never read her letters home), but the rebellious Fossey threw over her wealthy British fiancé to meet the challenge, and ended up on Rwanda's Mount Visoke.

With time she gained the gorillas' trust and became a respected expert on their behavior. She fought the loneliness of her mountain camp, Karisoke, by taking numerous lovers (including Leakey and married *National Geographic* photographer Bob Campbell) but gradually lost desire for human contact. ("The more you learn about the dignity of the gorilla," she remarked, "the more you want to avoid people.") What was once a scientific study degenerated into a personal vendetta against poachers who captured gorillas to sell to zoos or trophy hunters. She mercilessly interrogated suspects in her camp and was accused of using black magic to intimidate the locals. When Fossey, at 53, was found with her head split open by her own bush knife on December 26, 1985, the Rwandan government, whom she had often accused of selling out the rare species, said the naturalist had so many enemies they didn't know where to begin to look for her killer. ■

RACHEL CARSON

She warned it isn't nice to fool Mother Nature

SHE WISHED TO COME BACK IN ANOTHER LIFE AS A TERN—A BIRD that spends even more time at the seashore than Rachel Carson did herself. From walks with her mother in the woods of her native Pennsylvania, Carson grew up with a love of nature rivaled only by her love of the printed word. She went to college to study English but switched to marine biology. She first applied her talents as an editor for the federal Fish and Wildlife Service. From her experiences she wrote *The Sea Around Us,* a bestseller for 86 weeks that made her name as a lyrical writer and dedicated conservationist. Carson, who never married but raised her niece after her sister's death, left her job to write full-time. A friend in Massachusetts, seeing birds die from mosquito spray, gave Carson the impetus for her most noted work, *Silent Spring,* which awoke the nation to the dangers of pesticides: "One species—man—[has] acquired significant power to alter the nature of his world." Two years after its publication, Carson died of cancer, at age 56, having altered the world with her clarion call. ∎

"It was a black day when I took Pucker and Coco into the forest for the last time," she said, before the two (with Fossey in 1969) were sold to a zoo.

Fossey wrote she did "nothing terribly illegal" to protect her gorillas (in '71).

"Future generations are unlikely to condone our lack of prudent concern for the integrity of the natural world," wrote Carson (in 1962).

KATHARINE GRAHAM

*After her husband's suicide left her alone at the top,
she took command, raising the* Post *to new heights*

WHAT WE KNOW ABOUT WATERGATE, WE OWE NOT ONLY TO Woodward and Bernstein, but to the woman who had the guts to publish what they discovered about President Nixon and his cohorts. She stood up to threats of jail rather than hand over her reporters' notes to a judge, and would not budge even as the stock price of the Washington Post Co.—which held the newspaper her family had owned since the Depression—plummeted under attacks from the White House.

Just out of college, Katharine Meyer was offered a cushy job at the *Post* by her father, but chose to take a low-paying reporting position in San Francisco. Once she earned her spurs, she joined the *Post* and, in Washington, met and married Supreme Court clerk Phil Graham, with whom she had four children. The couple purchased the *Post* from her father for $1 million in 1948, and Phil acted as president until 1963, when, having suffered from lengthy bouts of depression, he committed suicide. Shattered, Graham, who had spent her married life as a homemaker, took over the reins despite being raised with "the assumption [that] women were intellectually inferior to men." Experience dispelled the notion, and the *Post* earned 17 Pulitzers in her 28 years. Graham, now 71, recently took that prize herself for her 1997 memoir of those years. ∎

"I have been credited with courage [in] Watergate," said Graham (in 1991). "I never felt there was much choice."

Jerry Seinfeld submitted to *The Barbara Walters Special* **in 1992.**

"Mummy doesn't drive. Mummy burns the meatloaf. All Mummy can do is television," Walters (at NBC in 1964) recalls her daughter's saying as a child.

BARBARA WALTERS

What kind of tree would she be? The tallest oak in the TV news forest

PEOPLE TALK ABOUT BARBARA WALTERS BEING driven. True on two counts: First, in just over a decade she went from writing copy to landing TV news's first million-dollar contract. Second, she can't drive a car; she is afraid to. But the Manhattan-based Walters travels with a production crew, so her fear of getting behind the wheel hasn't been a hindrance.

The once-shy daughter of a nightclub owner overcame far bigger hurdles to become the most prominent female telejournalist ever. Like, that voice. The soft *r*'s that mar her locution. (She hates to be teased about it, but once, when she had to say "Mount Ararat" on the air, she joked that she'd like to change it to "Mount Kisco.") And in her early career she faced undisguised sexism. As the *Today* Girl, in the '60s, she got the soft stories while her cohosts handled the news. She started doing interviews on location, so the plums couldn't be passed on to someone else, and turned the corner as the only

woman in the press corps that followed Richard Nixon to China. In 1977, ABC lured her with the now-famous contract for more money than any man had made in the business, pairing her on the evening news with Harry Reasoner, who didn't hide his contempt for her, even when she arranged the first joint interview with Egypt's Anwar Sadat and Israel's Menachem Begin.

Since then the thrice-divorced mother of one daughter has racked up one-on-ones with everyone from Fidel Castro and Boris Yeltsin to Barbra Streisand and Katharine Hepburn, who fielded the famous "What kind of tree?" question. Still coanchoring 20/20 twice a week and producing her eponymous specials, Walters no longer has to prove she can do what the boys can do and has launched an all-women morning show, *The View*. Now 66, she has no intention of bowing out. Said a former producer: "Barbara will die with the red light on." ■

Hopper (addressing the Phoenix Press Club in 1963) spent a tax-deductible $5,000 a year on her trademark hats.

HEDDA HOPPER

When she got a bee in her bonnet, it was the stars who got stung

On the advice of a numerologist, Hopper (with Cary Grant in 1944) changed her first name to Hedda.

A CTRESS JOAN BENNETT ONCE SENT HER A SKUNK. JOSEPH COTTEN WAS SO ENRAGED after she revealed his extramarital affair with Deanna Durbin that he approached her at a Hollywood event and kicked her, right through the gold party chair she sat on. For gossip columnist Hedda Hopper, it was all in a day's work: Her ability to make or break a movie career meant that she was at once avidly read, slavishly courted and widely despised in the industry. In their heyday she and archrival Louella Parsons, with a combined daily readership of 75 million, were the most powerful women in Hollywood.

Born Elda Furry in Hollidaysburg, Pennsylvania, in 1885, she quit school after eighth grade to join a theatrical troupe, then worked as a chorus girl in New York City. In 1913, at 28, she became the fifth wife of W. DeWolf Hopper, a matinee idol 27 years her senior. But as her film career took off and his sank, he increasingly taunted and cheated on her. In 1922 the couple, who had one son, divorced. By 1938, when she launched her column, *Hedda Hopper's Hollywood*, Hopper had acted in more than 100 pictures, and she always projected movie-star glamor, dressing in designer clothes—Mainbocher was a favorite—and reveling in the sumptuous Beverly Hills home she liked to call "the house that fear built."

Unable to type, Hopper dictated the dish she gathered from informants including milkmen, morticians and obstetricians. A feverish Commie hater, she decried racial intermixing and led the attack on Charlie Chaplin's promiscuity and leftist politics that drove him out of the United States. "Blessed with eternal middle age," as TIME put it, she worked until, at 80, she abruptly succumbed to double pneumonia. But her full life was apparently marred by loneliness. "Get married," Hopper once advised Margaret Sullivan. "Don't wind up an old lady in a big house like I am." ∎

EMILY POST

To the manners born, the wealthy socialite taught the middle class couth

HER WELL-BRED BALTIMORE FAMILY WAS APPALLED when she took the then-unthinkable step of divorcing her philandering banker husband, Edwin, and set off to raise two young sons as a single mother in turn-of-the-century New York City. Emily Price Post, a willowy brunette with Gibson Girl looks, whose architect father designed New York's exclusive Tuxedo Park, managed to parlay her blue-blooded background (finishing school, summers in Bar Harbor, Maine, and Europe) into society novels that earned enough to send offspring Bruce and Ned through Harvard. Though scorning existing books of good manners as pretentious ("Nothing," she once said, "is less important than which fork you use"), Post was cajoled into writing a commonsensible update. Her *Etiquette: The Blue Book of Social Usage* became an immediate best-seller when it appeared in 1922, appealing to a new middle class eager to make its way in society.

Just a few years after that triumph, she was devastated by the death of architect son Bruce but coped, continuing to turn out a column syndicated in over 200 newspapers and hosting a regular radio broadcast. So beloved was she for her effervescent personality and decidedly unstuffy advice that when Walter Winchell announced she was ill, 100 telegrams arrived within the hour. When she died at 86, in 1960, the dynasty continued. Peggy Post, the current incumbent, competes with sassier colleagues like Judith (Miss Manners) Martin and tackles thornier issues, like dealing with ethnic jokes and gay marriage. But, says Peggy of her great-grandmother-in-law: "I don't think she'd be thrown by today's etiquette questions. I think she would have moved along with the times." ■

"Etiquette is the science of living," maintained Post. She liked to work in bed after her coffee and zwieback.

MAGGIE KUHN

The Gray Panther bared fangs on behalf of 'old people'

MAGGIE KUHN'S LIFE WAS A SOCIAL STATEMENT RIGHT FROM THE WOMB. She was born in Buffalo because her radical mother had moved there to avoid raising children in the segregated South. A longtime activist herself, Kuhn founded the Gray Panthers in 1970, after being ousted from her secretarial job with the United Presbyterian Church at age 65. She coined the term ageism and successfully fought to overturn mandatory retirement laws and reform scandalous conditions in nursing homes. Her Panthers took on any and all indignities to old people (phrasing Kuhn preferred to senior citizens) including negative stereotypes in the media. Their founder never minced words, describing retirement communities as "big playpens for wrinkled babies" and exhorting her constituency to "have sex until rigor mortis sets in." She provided an example by her 15-year affair with a married minister, and by a dalliance with a college student. Never married herself, she described her crusade as "a pilgrimage but also a lark." Two weeks before she died, at 89, in 1995, Kuhn was still on the streets picketing, with striking transit workers in Philadelphia. ∎

In 1916 Sanger (center, with sister Ethel Byrne in background) bravely—and illegally—counseled women in a short-lived Brooklyn clinic.

"The older you get, the more outrageous you can be, because you have nothing to lose," said Kuhn (demonstrating in Washington in 1981).

MARGARET SANGER

She conceived a movement that gave women control of their reproductive destinies

I

T WAS PERHAPS INEVITABLE: AMERICA'S LEADING birth control proponent was one of 11 children. Born in Corning, New York, to a poor Irish tombstone cutter and his wife, Margaret Higgins was only 17 when her mother, Anne, died. Though the cause was TB, Margaret believed Anne had been worn out by childbirth.

Margaret was confirmed in her life's work 15 years later, after she had wed architect William Sanger, borne three children and moved to New York City. In 1912, while working as a visiting nurse among the poor, she watched a woman die after a self-induced abortion. Renouncing nursing, Sanger dedicated herself to giving women the means to control reproduction. She was confronting a profound taboo. Not even doctors provided contraceptive advice, and it was a federal crime to send such information by mail. In her single-minded fight to make birth control—her own term—legal, Sanger was arrested many times. In 1916 she and her sister opened, in Brooklyn, the nation's first birth control clinic. Before they were arrested and imprisoned 10 days later, nearly

500 women had paid the 10¢ registration fee. In 1921, Sanger founded the American Birth Control League, forerunner of Planned Parenthood.

Sanger was at heart a feminist, intent on liberating women from their role as "brood animal for the masculine civilizations of the world." Moreover she believed that birth control would permit the sort of lovemaking, "without consciousness of fear or consequence," depicted in popular romances. She herself took many lovers, among them writer H.G. Wells and pioneer sexologist Havelock Ellis. Divorced in 1920, she soon wed J. Noah H. Slee, millionaire maker of Three-in-One Oil, after forging a premarital agreement that guaranteed her sexual freedom and specified that she keep her name.

By 1966, when Sanger died at 86, millions of American women were taking the Pill, the development of which she had helped finance. The year before, the Supreme Court had upheld married people's right to contraceptive information—one more victory in her 50-year crusade: "Every child a wanted child." ∎

Creators

WHATEVER THEY CHOSE, TO AMAZE OR AMUSE, THEY ALWAYS FOLLOWED THEIR MUSE

worked as a ake dancer nightclubs, ry cook in mburger nts ... and ce had a job a mechanic's op," the poet '96) said of r early days.

MAYA ANGELOU

Love of language released her from her self-imposed cage of silence

T A DINNER IN 1994 THAT MAYA Angelou gave for Nobel laureate Toni Morrison, Oprah Winfrey remarked, "Maya has the ability to draw people together. You always know you're going to leave feeling more whole than when you came."

Angelou well understood the struggle to become whole. When she was 3, her own world was shattered as her parents divorced and she—then known as Marguerite Johnson—was sent to live with her grandparents in tiny Stamps, Arkansas. On a trip to San Francisco she was raped by her mother's boyfriend. When he was later murdered, after his release from prison, the whipsawing shocks sent the 8-year-old into a long period of self-imposed silence. It was then that Johnson developed her love of language, trying to turn her whole body into "an ear." Her silence ended when she was 13, after an English teacher told her that to appreciate poetry, she had to let it roll off her tongue.

Later it began to roll off her pen, beginning with her sonorous, 1970 autobiography *I Know Why the Caged Bird Sings* (the first of 14 books). That was well after she graduated from high school, eight months pregnant, became a madam of a whorehouse to support her illegitimate son and sang at San Francisco's hip Purple Onion (Maya was her stage name; first husband Tosh Angelou provided the rest). Now a professor at North Carolina's Wake Forest University, the poet often isolates herself in a local hotel room with a yellow legal pad, a Bible, a bottle of sherry and a deck of cards (solitaire gives her something to do with her hands while thinking). Writing, she says, is a painful process of "dragging my pencil across the old scars to sharpen it." The scars include three failed marriages ("I have lost good men," she mused, "because I have no middle passage"). But the strength and lyricism of her poetry earned her an invitation to compose and deliver a poem for President Clinton's 1993 Inauguration. ■

Though she wrote the song "Woodstock," Mitchell (in 1994) missed the festival due to airport trouble. "I watched it on TV," she said.

JONI MITCHELL

Folk and jazz conjoined in her sinuous spirit

S HE CITES EDITH PIAF AND BOB DYLAN AS INSPIRATION—AND you hear them both in her own elliptical, allusive compositions. Joni Mitchell has proven as adept at weaving tapestries of jazz and rock as at stitching complex stories on the clean cloth of her acoustic guitar. And her songs have stood up to renderings by others: covered by Judy Collins and Frank Sinatra, sampled by Janet Jackson.

Born in Alberta, Canada, Roberta Joan Anderson suffered from polio at 9 and later taught herself guitar. A year out of high school she married Chuck Mitchell, a musician she had known for three days, and divorced him after a year. Unknown and broke when she got pregnant, she gave up a daughter for adoption. (She later married and divorced producer Larry Klein, and was reunited with her daughter in 1995.) She then hit the New York folk scene. Discovered by David Crosby, she launched a career that hit early highs with *Blue* and *Court and Spark*. In the 1980s she explored all the music curiosity led her to, including African rhythms, even if fans or critics didn't follow. Still, Mitchell, now 54, does not seem to miss the early days when she was idolized. Says she: "I slept through that queendom." ∎

"I never said there wasn't some of me in the songs," says Mitchell (in 1968).

DIANA VREELAND

For 50 years, it wasn't fashion until she said it was fashion

T HE BIKINI IS ONLY THE MOST IMPORtant invention since the atom bomb." To say something like that and get away with it takes special conviction and aplomb. Diana Vreeland had both. She knew not only what fashion should be, but how to persuade women to accept her vision as if it possessed the logic of a mathematical equation. "Pink is the navy-blue of India!" came the word from her poppy-red-painted mouth. And so it was.

Born in Paris to a Scottish stockbroker and his American wife, Diana Dalziel received little classroom education, but she had unrivaled exposure to the cultured class at her parents' salons, which included Nijinsky and Isadora Duncan. While on vacation in New York, Diana met banker Thomas Vreeland, whom she married in 1924. When the couple moved in 1936 to New York City, she found his salary would not keep them and their two sons in the style to which Diana wished them to grow accustomed, so she took a job writing for *Harper's Bazaar*. There she offered audacious suggestions for lux living, like, "Why not turn your ermine into a bathrobe?" She was named editor within three years and remained dedicated to the magazine until 1962, when she left for its rival *Vogue*.

Vogue was her bully pulpit—her flock, in her words, "the beautiful people." She ordained many models and designers as stars: Marisa Berenson, Verushka, Twiggy, Halston, Oscar de la Renta, Bill Blass and photographer Richard Avedon. When recession hit, in 1971, she was ignominiously fired. Vreeland died in '89 (at eightysomething, she never gave her age), leaving a fashion press that still bears her theatrical mark and follows her haute adjure, like, "Never fear being vulgar—just boring, middle-class or dull." ∎

Vreeland (in 1983) said her favorite lunch was a peanut-butter-and-honey sandwich on whole wheat, a shot of Scotch, a vitamin B-12 injection and ice cream, but not in a round scoop because that made it "a bore to eat."

"My career was planned," said Mary Pickford (with director Ernst Lubitsch in 1923). "There was never anything accidental about it."

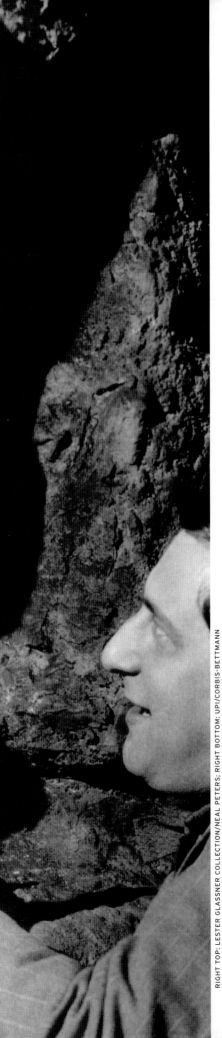

MARY PICKFORD

She played a moppet, but the lady made herself a mogul

B Y THE AGE OF 5, GLADYS SMITH WAS PLAYING BIT PARTS AT TORONTO'S Princess Theatre, and at 8, the valiant young performer became her family's chief breadwinner when her alcoholic father deserted the household and her mother couldn't cope. Like the spunky tyros she usually portrayed, Pickford escaped life's perils by relentlessly pressing ahead. Arranging her own publicity shots, she eventually graduated to starring roles. She broke onto Broadway by plucking the heartstrings of director David Belasco, telling him she was "the father of my family." In 1909, D.W. Griffith ushered her onto her first movie set, offering a mere $5 a day. By now a shrewd veteran, the 16-year-old, coached by her enterprising mother, asked for $10—and got it. Soon America's Sweetheart was telling rival director Adolph Zukor, "I can't afford to work for only $10,000 a week."

Her natural ease on-camera, topped by the curly ringlets later imitated by Shirley Temple, swept away the staginess then in vogue and made her the world's first great film celebrity. In London she caused such huge traffic jams that King George V was once stalled in a limo for 20 minutes. Back home, fans eagerly monitored the doings at Pickfair, the mansion she shared with second husband Douglas Fairbanks Sr. There the couple dined off gold plates with the likes of Albert Einstein and Amelia Earhart. Already

Pickford (with Charlie Chaplin, left, and husband Douglas Fairbanks Sr. in 1921) founded the United Artists studio.

pulling down the industry's heftiest paycheck (about $500,000 a year), Pickford went on to become the most powerful woman in the business when she, Charlie Chaplin, Fairbanks and Griffith formed United Artists in 1919.

Wary of being pigeonholed (as Chaplin had been with the Little Tramp), Pickford said of her waifish signature roles in *Pollyanna* and *Rebecca of Sunnybrook Farm,* "The 'little girl' made me. I wasn't waiting for the 'little girl' to kill me." Yet audiences didn't accept her in provocative roles (though she won her only Oscar in 1929 for *Coquette*). Forgettable in talkies, she bowed out at 40. Lillian Gish prevailed upon her not to burn her films, but Pickford never seemed to grasp her significance in movie history. She spent her later years hitting the bottle and picking on her third husband, actor Buddy Rogers, and died, at 86, in 1979, a bitter recluse. ■

Early poverty taught Pickford the value of a dollar. Sam Goldwyn once said, "It took longer to make one of Mary's contracts than it did to take one of Mary's pictures." But she didn't mind volunteering at a California Army canteen in 1942.

Her films were "not only about women's problems," said Lupino (in 1956). "They were definitely about men's too."

IDA LUPINO

Feminine, but not feminist, she was nevertheless a pioneer in Hollywood

IDA LUPINO, THE SCION OF LONDON VAUDE-villians, came to Hollywood in 1933, and by 1940 she was touted by Warner Brothers as the next Bette Davis. But after some 50 films, including *High Sierra* and *Road House*, and type-cast as the "tough moll with the heart of gold," she formed a production company with second husband Collier Young to seek more interesting roles. Her real breakthrough came in a picture about teen pregnancy, *Not Wanted*, in 1948, when the director got sick. His name remained in the credits, but it was Lupino's vision that saw the project through. She became the only woman director of note in her time and arguably the first female Hollywood "hyphenate" (she also wrote and pro-duced). But rather than flaunt her power, Lupino soft-pedaled it on the principle that "men hate bossy women." Instead her public persona was that of a charming smart aleck. When she and her third husband, actor Howard Duff, divorced after 32 years of marriage, the last 11 spent apart, some-one asked Lupino what took her so long. "I finally got off my duff, darling," she replied.

Lupino brought the lens of her gender to films about rape (*Outrage*, 1950) and cheating men (*The Bigamist*, 1953) as well as to the acclaimed action thriller (*The Hitchhiker*, 1953) and dozens of TV episodes, from *Have Gun, Will Travel* to *The Untouchables*. She was undoubtedly a trailblazer, but also an anomaly; her success did not immedi-ately pave the way for female directors to match the numbers of their male counterparts. "Any woman who wishes to smash into the world of men isn't very feminine," she once told a reporter. "Baby, we can't go smashing." When she died, at age 77, of a stroke and colon cancer in 1995, the Motion Picture Academy had recognized only one woman (Italy's Lina Wertmuller, in 1976) with a Best Director Oscar nomination. Today it has yet to bestow the award on a woman. ∎

DOROTHEA LANGE

She gave a face to the Depression's overlooked

*A*S THE PRIME EARNER IN A FAMILY of four (her husband, Maynard Dixon, was a painter), photographer Dorothea Lange made her living making portraits of wealthy San Franciscans. But when the country fell into economic trauma in the 1930s, she quit her lucrative career. Working with the economist Paul Taylor, she began photographing migrant workers for the California State Emergency Relief Administration, drawing attention to their shameful housing conditions. When the Farm Security Administration aimed to record the lives of farmers, Lange made portraits of sharecroppers, dust bowl migrants and the otherwise invisible people struck hardest by poverty. She believed the camera, rather than an indulgence, was "an instrument that teaches people how to see without a camera." Lange prided herself on "not taking anything away from anyone: their privacy, their dignity, their wholeness." In 1935, Lange divorced Dixon and married Taylor, her partner in this passionate calling.

Lange had much in common with her Depression-era subjects. Born in blue-collar Hoboken, New Jersey, she survived a childhood bout of polio that left her with a lifelong limp. When she was 12, her father, a lawyer, abandoned the family. Prowling Manhattan as a teen, keenly observing the life of the city, she vowed to become a photographer. In 1966 the Museum of Modern Art gave her a retrospective—the first ever for a woman. But Lange, who had designed the exhibit in 1964, died of cancer, at 70, three months before the opening. ■

To be a valuable photographer, thought Lange (in Texas in 1934), "you go in over your head, not just up to your neck."

GRANDMA MOSES

After tilling the soil most of her days, she began to till memory in paint

HER LIFE SPANNED ABRAHAM LINCOLN to the Lincoln Continental, the family farm to the elite art world of Manhattan. She lived 101 years but is known for her surprising accomplishments in only the last 23. Having left school at age 12, given birth to 10 children (just five of whom lived beyond infancy) and labored with her husband, Thomas Moses, on dairy farms in Virginia and Upstate New York, Anna Mary Robertson picked up a paintbrush at 78 because her arthritic hands couldn't farm or do needlework any longer.

Self-taught, she was selling her oil-on-recycled-wood paintings in 1938 at a shop in rural New York when a dealer happened upon them. He bought them all and asked to meet the artist. By 1940, Grandma Moses, as she was dubbed by a critic and subsequently called in the press, was showing at Manhattan's Museum of Modern Art and in a one-person gallery show titled, "What a Farmwife Painted."

Her only training had been to copy Currier & Ives prints, but she quickly grew to be regarded as an American master. (She sold her paintings for as much as $1,000; today they can fetch $70,000.) The instant appeal of her naïve work was its link to another era. Her memories provided her inspiration. She depicted homespun scenes: apple picking, quilting bees, tapping maple trees for syrup, and the northeastern winters that brought towns to a peaceful, pristine standstill.

What seemed a late-blooming interest in art was actually a passion that dated from her girlhood but had been suppressed for most of her hard-toiling life. At age 92 she wrote, "I

was quite small, my father would get me and my brothers white paper by the sheet. He liked to see us draw pictures, it was a penny a sheet and it lasted longer than candy." Grandma Moses would enjoy the sweetness of rendering her imagination in paint for another eight years before her death, in 1961. ∎

Moses (at 100) made more than a thousand paintings, but her granddaughter remembers the family's watching her work and saying, "Oh, for heaven's sake!"

M.F.K. FISHER

A hunger for the sensuous fueled a literary feast amid hardships

OOD WAS JUST ONE OF THE PASSIONS that consumed the gastronomic maverick whom British-born poet W.H. Auden called "America's greatest writer." M.F.K. Fisher's love of words was inspired by her father, a quirky newspaper editor who led his Michigan family cross-country ("We could have been called hippies," Fisher said, "had the word been invented in 1912") before settling in Whittier, California. Marriage to fellow UCLA student Al Fisher let Mary Frances Kennedy exchange America's bland custards and stewed tomatoes for the earthly delights of Dijon, France, where her husband earned his doctorate (and she was photographed by Man Ray). There Fisher learned about such delicacies as oysters that were "so fresh," she wrote, "their delicate flanges drew back at your breath upon them."

The experience heightened all her senses. After the couple returned to the U.S., Fisher found her true soulmate, Dillwyn Parrish (painter Maxfield's cousin). The two later ran off to Switzerland, marrying in 1938 after her divorce and the publication of her first book, *Serve It Forth*. But in 1941 disaster struck at home and abroad: Parrish died (Mary Frances later married, and divorced, book publisher Donald Friede, raising her two daughters alone), and the U.S. plunged into WW II. She coped by writing the witty survival guide *How to Cook a Wolf*. But the same brilliance that had transformed the once-pedestrian genre of food writing into an art fanned accusations that the author was tackling too insignificant a subject. She said, "When I write of hunger, I'm writing about love, and the hunger for it." Fisher's own appetites never abated. Food critic Ruth Reichl recalled seeing her the year before she died of Parkinson's, at 83: "Eyesight failing, voice gone, fingers unable to hold a pen, she was reduced to little more than her own ferocious energy. But there she was, face made-up, propped up on her pillows. She sipped a cocktail through a straw, and nibbled at a plate of oysters." ∎

John Updike saluted her as the "poet of the appetites." Maya Angelou said that, at 74, Fisher (at her Sonoma Valley home in 1982) was "still as sensual as mocha cheesecake."

"You take a chance when you are an artist," says Bourgeois (in 1991), "not to be understood at all."

LOUISE BOURGEOIS

A childhood with mother, father and father's mistress bred an exorcism in art

WHEN THE MUSEUM OF MODERN ART IN NEW York City gave a retrospective exhibition of Louise Bourgeois's career in 1982, the sculptor and mixed-media artist, then 70, was largely unknown. Yet for 50 years, with rare ferocity and independence, she had been exploring subjects like female identity, the body and the fractured family, long before society or the art world were ready to pronounce them hot-button topics. With her MOMA retrospective, the woman who had worked with Léger in France in the '30s, and had later befriended Marcel Duchamp and other artists, finally came into her own. "Her work is charged with tenderness and violence, acceptance and defiance, ambivalence and conviction," said *The New York Times*. Wrote the critic Kay Larson: "A new generation . . . has discovered a living pioneer and role model." In 1992 the artist was chosen to represent the U.S. at the prestigious Venice Biennale.

Bourgeois had stemmed from ironically bourgeois roots. Her parents restored carpets and tapestries, and from age 10 she learned art by drawing in missing details from damaged pieces. It was a comfortable existence, and Louise was praised for her ability. But serenity was poisoned by the presence of her father's live-in mistress, who doubled as Louise's tutor. Much of her art, both on paper and in metal, marble and even found animal parts, was an attempt to come to terms with her father's betrayal of the family. Early pictures dealt with domesticity, depicting women's bodies with houses where a head should be. Later she constructed cages that suggested either wombs or prisons. "My pieces are made out of exorcism," she has said, "things that are bothering me and I have to get rid of." Now 86, the widowed mother of three sons continues to work and live in New York. "My goal," she has said, "is to find equilibrium between extremes, a sense of balance." ∎

SIMONE DE BEAUVOIR

The author of The Second Sex *put 'freedom and frankness' first*

In 1970, de Beauvoir and Sartre hawked copies of his left-wing newspaper in the streets of Paris after it had been banned by the government. The couple were later arrested.

IT'S IRONIC THAT ONE OF THE WORLD'S LEADING feminist voices—a woman Betty Friedan and Gloria Steinem praise as a major influence—should be linked inexorably to a more famous man. But the French writer, teacher and philosopher Simone de Beauvoir would have seen no contradiction in that reality. She lived her life as an example of how women could escape the trap of societal inferiority that she described in her 1949 landmark work, *The Second Sex*. She never married or lived with her lover, the philosopher Jean Paul Sartre, maintaining her independence and her own residence in Paris from the time they met as students until his death in 1980. For 51 years she was his intellectual equal and romantic foil, and both enjoyed "contingent" relationships on the side. Hers, which included American novelist Nelson Algren and filmmaker Claude (*Shoah*) Lanzmann as well as lesbian liaisons, became material for de Beauvoir's novels. She once described the arrangement with Sartre, saying, "We have pioneered our own relationship—its freedom, intimacy and frankness." Her devotion to the couple's shared tenets of existentialism developed early—well before her years with Sartre—during her adolescence at Catholic school. As a girl she had rebelled against the religion and middle-class values of her mother, and by age 14 she felt confident that there was no God.

She was 41 when *The Second Sex* was published. The book set forth an unprecedented analysis of the state of women, as well as radical solutions to the problems of inequity in society: "Let [women] be provided with living strength of their own, let them have the means to attack the world and wrest from it their own subsistence, and their dependence will be abolished." When de Beauvoir died at 78 of pneumonia, in 1986, she was buried in a grave in Montparnasse with the ashes of Sartre. "Of the two," said a professor who knew them both, "it is she who is the philosopher." ■

JACQUELINE SUSANN

Not just playing with dolls, she made trash legit in sex-drugs-and-power potboilers

IN 1963, JACQUELINE SUSANN, A 44-YEAR-OLD writer and onetime actress recovering from a radical mastectomy, made a pact with God: Give me 10 more years, and I'll settle for being a bestselling author. On pink paper on a pink IBM Selectric, she started typing out a novel titled *Valley of the Dolls*. When the work came out in 1966, Susann left nothing to chance. She undertook a blizzard-like national tour virtually unprecedented at the time but now the promotional norm. "There was a time when I was doing 10 shows a day, 18 interviews a day. I was killing myself," she said. "But I made it." Despite the mastectomy the cancer returned, but not before Susann got her wish. When she died at 56, in 1974, *Dolls* was the top-selling novel of all time, with worldwide sales of more than 28 million copies. "The phenomenon of celebrity books didn't exist

as we know it," says Michael Korda, who edited Susann's third effort (and second No. 1), 1969's *The Love Machine*. "Jackie threw the whole business open to a lot of things that had not been possible to do in book publishing."

Susann's partner in her quest was her husband, press agent Irving Mansfield—a kindhearted man unlike the cruel, domineering executives of her books. While Susann and Mansfield gamely coped with her cancer, they mourned the fate of their autistic son, Guy, who was institutionalized at age 4. They faithfully visited Guy nearly every weekend and kept both tragedies private, even from friends. "Jackie would leave her treatment and not be well, put her makeup on and go directly to a book party," recalled Mansfield's stepdaughter Lisa Bishop. Susann may have loved multiple four-letter words, but self-pity was not among them. ∎

GERTRUDE STEIN

She showed her famous acolytes a genius is a genius is a . . .

ER BROTHER LEO CALLED HER work "godalmighty rubbish," but Gertrude Stein advised those placing her in the literary firmament to "think of the Bible and Homer, think of Shakespeare and think of me." Both had their points. Though her endlessly repetitive novels were virtually unreadable (Wyndham Lewis called her writing "a cold, black suet pudding"), her innovative use of words blazed the way for writers like James Joyce. And her charming *The Autobiography of Alice B. Toklas* (actually a biography of Stein by Stein) became a bestseller still popular today. What remains inarguable is Stein's influential role in the lives of artists from Picasso (he called her Pard, a term that he got from westerns) to Hemingway ("Gertrude Stein and me are just like brothers") to F. Scott Fitzgerald. In her Paris salon, hung with Matisses and Cézannes she'd acquired for a pittance, the American expatriate debated the fledgling modern movement with the male geniuses (*"moi aussi,* perhaps," she hoped) who sat at her feet, while her partner, Alice Babette Toklas, entertained their wives. Stein, daughter of a San Francisco cable-car magnate, had settled in Paris after her love for a Bryn Mawr grad went unrequited. Not so with Alice B., who stayed by her side, typing her nearly illegible manuscripts, until cancer took her in 1946, at 72. "Oh, Gertrude, what is the answer?" Toklas implored of Stein on her deathbed. Ever cryptic, Stein replied, "What is the question?" ∎

"What women want to read about is lust," noted writer Nora Ephron. "And Jacqueline Susann gave it to them." (In 1970 she referred to a chart she had made of her characters in *The Love Machine.*)

Stein's partner, Alice B. Toklas (right, in 1944), was a world-renowned chef, but her 1954 cookbook is best-remembered for its recipe for hash fudge.

THEIR PASSION LIFTED OTHERS, OFTEN AT THEIR OWN EXPENSE

tragic HEROINES

marilyn MONROE

*Ticking within
the blonde bombshell,
the heart of a little-girl-lost longed for protection*

"I enjoy acting when you really hit it right," said Monroe (on the set of *The Misfits*) in 1962. "And I guess I've always had too much fantasy to be only a housewife. Well, also, I had to eat."

EVEN BEFORE HER DEATH AT 36, MARILYN MONROE HAD GROWN absurdly easy to imitate: Don a platinum wig, dab on a beauty mark beside bright-red lips, adopt a kittenish voice. And yet, Monroe was inimitable. Obscured by the caricature was a person, with flaws, fears and frustrated dreams. Her half sister told LIFE that Marilyn's sexy walk was the result of her having one leg slightly shorter than the other, that her beauty mark was a mole she colored in with an eye pencil, and that she had longed desperately for children.

She was born Norma Jean Mortenson to a single mother, Gladys Baker (née Monroe), and once said she had known she wanted to be an actress from age 5. Her mother had spent years in mental hospitals; Monroe, raised in foster families, learned she was born out-of-wedlock only when she applied for her first marriage license at 16. (Her second marriage, to baseball legend Joe DiMaggio, took place when she was 28; the third, to playwright Arthur Miller, two years later.) Whether her family's history of depression presaged Monroe's pill addiction and fatal barbiturate overdose is but part of the legend picked over by everyone from Norman Mailer to Gloria Steinem. Monroe left behind a lot to wonder about: the truth of her supposed affairs with both Robert and Jack Kennedy, what kind of mother she would have been to the child she and then-husband Miller conceived and lost to miscarriage, and what direction her career might have taken. Not in question is the solid work she left behind: sparkling comic performances (*Gentlemen Prefer Blondes, Some Like It Hot*) as well as the fragile and affecting (*Bus Stop, The Misfits*). Monroe, who studied drama even after she became a star, could not escape the tag of sex symbol. "That's the trouble—a sex symbol becomes a thing," she said a week before her death in 1962. "I just hate to be a thing. But if I'm going to be a symbol of something, I'd rather have it be sex than some other things they've got symbols of." ∎

judy
GARLAND

Safe in the arms of an audience,
she basked in love that eluded her in life

"SHE IS NO VENUS, LET US ADMIT IT," WROTE A critic of Judy Garland as her star began to rise, "but how delightful is her smile, how genuine her emotion, how sure her timing, and how brilliantly she brings off her effects." Young Frances Gumm had the God-given talent to succeed, but nothing was left to chance by her notorious stage mother, Ethel Gumm, who landed Judy a contract at MGM in 1935, the year she turned 13 and her father died. Her mother's expectations and the studio's demands pushed Judy to early fame, then pushed her over the edge: She would run from *Andy Hardy* shoots with Mickey Rooney to her psychiatrist's couch. And at 16, when she was making *The Wizard of Oz*, she couldn't get through a day without uppers or sleep at night without downers.

"People en masse have always been wonderful to me," Garland said in 1961. "I truly have great love for an audience." One-on-one, however, her relationships were less satisfying. Her first marriage, to composer David Rose, lasted only three years. A year later she married director Vincente Minnelli, with whom she made *Meet Me in St. Louis*. They had one child, Liza, and divorced. Garland then married producer Sid Luft. They had a daughter, Lorna, and a son, Joseph, and also divorced. Those unhappy unions were marked by suicide attempts, time in sanatoriums, continued pill addiction and alcoholism. In spite of these trials—or perhaps, in part, because of them—Garland offered up stunning performances in films like *A Star Is Born*. Mickey Deans, a nightclub owner, is the only husband from whom she didn't split: In 1969 he found her dead, in their London home, from what the coroner declared "an incautious dose of barbituates."■

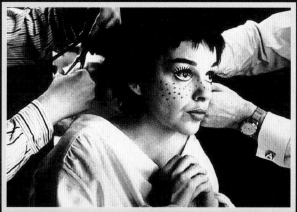

Producers, said Garland (watching rushes of *Lily Mars* in 1943), wanted her to be "the girl next door. But they couldn't find the right house or the right door." Inset: Getting primped for *A Star Is Born* in 1954.

edith
PIAF

*France's Little
Sparrow soared until illness
and heartbreak stilled her song*

D ELIVERED, AS SHE TOLD IT, IN A Paris gutter in 1915 by two gendarmes, Edith Gassion was soon abandoned by her parents and raised by prostitutes in her grandmother's brothel. Returning to the streets to sing, the teenager impressed a boîte impresario and, then, Maurice Chevalier. His opinion was seconded by tout Paris, which swooned over the frail chanteuse with the robust voice. She ran through three husbands and countless lovers, including a "terribly hurt" Yves Montand. But when her true love, boxer Marcel Cerdan, died in a 1949 plane crash, she never got over it. Injuries in three car wrecks— two with Charles Aznavour, whose career she launched—left her addicted to pills. Piaf's waiflike body could not take the strain, and three years after introducing her signature song, "Je Ne Regrette Rien" (No Regrets), the plucky singer Parisiens called The Kid succumbed to liver disease at age 47. ∎

dorothy
DANDRIDGE

Oscar came calling, but film racism doomed her career

"She was the right person in the right place at the wrong time," said Belafonte of Dandridge.

OROTHY DANDRIDGE WAS JUST 4 when her starstruck mother ditched her draftsman father for a lesbian lover and hightailed it from Cleveland to L.A. There she sang in a children's act and got a bit part in the Marx Brothers' *A Day at the Races*. Back East to perform at Harlem's Cotton Club, the then 19-year-old femme fatale met and married dancer Harold Nicholas. When their daughter was born brain-damaged, a distraught Dandridge blamed herself, and, bitter over Nicholas's womanizing, divorced him and returned to movies. Otto Preminger (who later became her lover) cast her opposite Harry Belafonte in 1954's *Carmen Jones*, for which she became the first black nominated for a Best Actress Oscar. That led to a trailblazing, interracial romance in *Island in the Sun* but mostly to frustrating stereotyped roles like the slave girl in *The King and I* (she declined). After a disastrous marriage to a Vegas hustler, she lost her Hollywood Hills home and was forced to institutionalize her daughter. Then Dandridge herself suffered alcohol problems and had a breakdown, and in 1965 she was found dead of a drug overdose, at 42, with $2.14 to her once luminous name. ∎

At New York City's Met, in 1956, she played *Norma*, an opera Callas once quit mid-performance with Italy's president in the audience.

maria

*Dubbed La Divina,
the soprano lived and sang like the very devil*

T HE HEROINE OF CHERUBINI'S OPERA *Medea* is a sorceress who avenges her betraying husband by murdering their children. Maria Callas, the mercurial diva who made Medea a signature role and starred in Pier Paolo Pasolini's non-singing 1970 movie adaptation, never went to that mythological or operatic excess. But her life could have inspired the grandest and saddest libretto, its turbulent trajectory taking her from ugly duckling to unparalleled prima donna and jet-set luminary and then, finally, to neglected recluse.

In some ways, Callas never escaped her own family melodrama. Born in 1923 to poor Greek parents in New York City, Maria was unwanted by her mother, who refused to look at her second daughter for four days after her birth. All affection was lavished on her sister Jackie. Fat, ungainly and nearsighted, Maria began music lessons at age 8, developing her uncommonly gifted voice and commanding dramatic presence for a professional debut at 17. Dark and striking, she slimmed along the way from 200 pounds to 130, and for 25 years the troubled and troublesome singer earned her sobriquet La Divina. "Pure electricity," exulted Leonard Bernstein. At the same time, Callas terrorized colleagues with legendary fits. "Of course I am difficult," she once conceded. "But I am not a monster."

By 1949 she had married Milanese businessman and opera buff Giovanni Meneghini, 26 years her senior. He offered stability, financial security and shrewd career management. Then, a decade later, Callas became smitten with Aristotle Onassis on a cruise. So much for Meneghini. "I was kept in a cage," she said of the marriage. "When I met Aristo and his friends, so full of life and glamor, I became a different woman." Meneghini's retort: "I created Callas, and she repaid my love by stabbing me in the back."

After what a society-page writer called "the most publicized love affair since Héloïse and Abelard," Onassis stunned the world by marrying Jackie Kennedy. "First I lost my weight, then I lost my voice, and now I've lost Onassis," Callas declared, but she later was to say that the shipping tycoon "will always be my best friend." She spent her last years mostly in her Paris flat, teaching occasional master classes and picking over the past. "Loneliness is emptiness, and that is nothing," she said. "It is worse than nothing." Callas died alone in her bed of a heart attack in 1977. She was 53. ∎

After receiving a summons, in a contractual lawsuit, at Chicago's Civic Opera House, Callas bellowed with her *bellissima* lyric pipes at the U.S. marshal who had served it.

frida KAHLO

Painting transformed her pain into a gift

I PAINT MY OWN REALITY." FRIDA Kahlo's reality was unforgiving, but like an alchemist she turned suffering into beauty. Born in Mexico City in 1907, Kahlo was struck early by polio. When she was 18, her spine was shattered in a trolley car accident. From her sickbed, she began painting and found love and a mentor in muralist Diego Rivera. In 1929 they married, but Rivera took many lovers, among them Frida's own sister. Kahlo had retaliatory liaisons with Leon Trotsky and others. She and Rivera divorced, but he begged her to remarry, and she accepted. In 1953 she wrote in her diary, "In spite of my long illness, I feel immense joy in LIVING." Enduring some 30 operations, she continued painting her brilliantly colored self-portraits, which depicted her broken body and heart. Yet a year and a half later, with suicidal musings in her journal, Kahlo was dead at 47, officially of pulmonary embolism. ∎

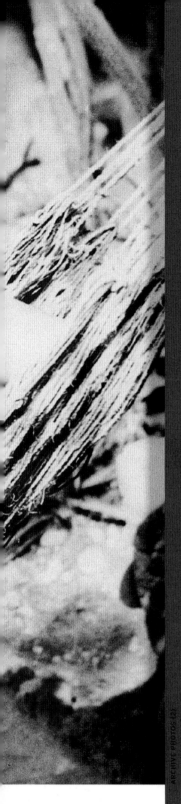

virginia WOOLF

Psychologically astute, she freed the novel to dream

VIRGINIA WOOLF EXISTED IN A SEA OF DEPRESSION. WRITING WAS BOTH her life raft and the weight that pulled her under. Even while creating some of the most innovative novels of Western literature, she endured a suicidal malaise. With unprecedented accuracy, Woolf recreated the language of thought, particularly women's, in books like *Mrs. Dalloway.* Work was an outlet for some of her anxiety, but the process also plunged her into what she called "the madness."

From childhood, in turn-of-the-century London, Virginia Stephen was well-cared-for by a father who nurtured a love of reading. When her mother died, Woolf had a nervous breakdown, at age 13. She was, writes Quentin Bell of his aunt, sexually abused by a half brother. After their father's death she and her brother Thoby and sister Vanessa Bell became the center of the intellectual circle later called the Bloomsbury Group, made up mainly of Thoby's friends from Cambridge. There she met critic Leonard Woolf. Together they founded a small press to publish her work and that of their friends. In 1912 they entered into a loving but sexless marriage. They remained together even as she took up with writer Vita Sackville-West. Despite great professional recognition and the devotion of a husband and lover, Woolf never overcame her profound sadness. In 1941 the 59-year-old author filled her pockets with garden stones, slipped into a river and drowned herself. ■

"Death was defiance," said a Woolf title character, Clarissa Dalloway. "Death was an attempt to communicate."

She seemed to reveal herself in each self-portrait, but Kahlo (at home in Mexico City) called herself *la gran ocultadora* (the great concealer).

ARCHIVE PHOTOS (2)

NINE LIVES

1974

Rocker husband Gregg Allman was "a mistake" she left after nine days. They had a son, Elijah.

NO QUESTION: WOMEN HAVE ALWAYS HAD TO BE RESILIENT, BUT THESE INDOMITABLE DAMES ARE THE MOTHERS OF REINVENTION

1960s

Cher finally seemed to make peace with Sonny Bono, her mentor and tormentor, after his fatal 1998 skiing accident.

"If grass can grow through cement," she mused from long experience, "love can find you at every time in your life."

1983

1988

1990

cting with Meryl
treep in *Silkwood*
roved her dimension
eyond the ditsiness.

It seemed inevitable that
Cher would lend her name
to a fragrance and label it
Uninhibited.

Asked who is the real Cher,
she said, "They all are."
Now she gets laser treatments
to erase her tattoos.

1996

Cher

*She was and is pop culture's
Unfinished Symphony*

SOMEONE ONCE SAID, 'THE ONLY thing that's gonna be left after a nuclear holocaust is Cher and cockroaches,'" the singer/actress observed in 1994. "I kind of think that's funny 'cause, you know, I am a survivor. If I am anything, that's what I am."

Indeed, at 52, she has transformed herself from teen runaway to half of the Flower Power pop-duo Sonny and Cher to Las Vegas showwoman to Oscar-winning actress to platinum-selling recording artist and infomercial pitchmeister. Along the way she has repeatedly changed her look (she admits to having had her breasts augmented and her nose reduced through plastic surgery) as well as the men in her life. "I can't keep doing the same thing over and over," she said in 1991. "I get bad at it, and I don't want to be bad."

But even as a child growing up in California's San Fernando Valley (Mom was a sometime model and singer; she left Dad when Cher was an infant), Cher—née Cherilyn Sarkisian—*did* want to be famous. Her first taste of stardom came in 1965, when, with future husband Sonny Bono, she scored with the hippie love song "I Got You, Babe." When their younger fans turned toward edgier acts, the duo traded their bell-bottoms for sequins and took their act first to the nightclub circuit and then to television with *The Sonny and Cher Comedy Hour*. After divorcing Bono in 1975 (their one daughter, Chastity, 29, is now a gay-rights activist), Cher initially returned to Vegas as a solo act. But in fear of "becoming the next Dinah Shore," she changed course again, trying her hand at acting. After critically acclaimed performances in the films *Silkwood* and *Mask*, Cher took home an Oscar for her work as the Brooklyn bookkeeper liberated by love in the 1987 romantic comedy *Moonstruck*. "Unless you risk looking foolish," she would later say, "you never have the possibility of being great." ∎

1967
Being cast by then-husband Roger Vadim as a sci-fi sex bomb in *Barbarella* raised Fonda's consciousness and hastened the end of their union and her evolution into what she called "a revolutionary woman."

Jane Fonda

Political activism and image morphing were, unlike her fitness tapes, no sweat

1971

Fonda won the first of her two Oscars for her portrayal of a prostitute in *Klute* (above) and took the other for 1978's *Coming Home.*

1972

On Radio Hanoi she broadcast to U.S. airmen to stop bombing North Vietnam. Several congressmen suggested that Fonda be tried for treason.

"GO FOR THE BURN" WAS BOTH THE DICTUM OF HER workout videos and the philosophy behind her full, volatile and passionate life path. From light-hearted ingenue to vinyl-clad temptress to earnest actress to peace activist to fitness guru, Jane Fonda made sliding out of an old skin and into a new one look easy. But the shift from sweet to sexy meant breaking, at least in the public's eye, from her esteemed actor father, Henry. And the metamorphosis from sex symbol to an anti-Vietnam war protester included a divorce from French director Roger Vadim and marriage to left-wing California politician Tom Hayden, which also eventually fell apart (she had one child by each). Becoming the shape-up queen of the '80s required a tricky balancing act between the seemingly shallow role of video gym teacher and the most substantive parts of her film career, including *On Golden Pond*, which costarred her dad and signaled their reconciliation.

Now living a comparatively quiet, married-lady life with media mogul Ted Turner, Fonda may appear to have burned out, or copped out, at 60. She no longer acts in films or takes high-profile ideological stands. But with Turner, who like Fonda lost a parent to suicide, she remains an important philanthropist and advocate, most recently for teen-pregnancy prevention. And Fonda still suffers the barbs of critics of her choices, from the right-wingers who never stop thinking of her as Hanoi Jane to feminists who decry her breast implants and her swanning around on Turner's arm. "Change," she told *Vanity Fair* by way of answer in 1997, "is the hardest thing in the world, and it's the first thing I look for in people." ■

Fonda created 23 hot-selling workout videos on her mission to reform what she labeled "institutionalized couch potatoes."

1983

Fonda has described Ted Turner, her husband since 1991, as a lot like her father but with "none of the bad parts. Ted is not afraid of expressing his need. And he loves women."

1980

1990

Tom Hayden, a radical-left lawyer who became a state senator, wed Fonda in 1973. The pair (on their solar-powered ranch with son Troy) adopted a girl from a troubled home who had attended a camp they ran.

1985
Her distinctive blend of lingerie, crucifixes and killer abs spawned dance-pop hits (and concern from some parents and Christian leaders) as well as a new breed of preteen: the Madonna Wanna-Be.

Madonna

Like a perpetual virgin, she kept renewing her assault on the public's attention span

To UNDERSTAND THE MOTHER, LOOK AT THE daughter. "I can see she is going to have my personality," Madonna said when Lourdes Ciccone Leon was two months old. "She has a strong will. All babies cry when they're hungry, but mine really makes it known what she wants." So too did Madonna when, not yet finished with college, she left Michigan for New York City. She wanted a record contract. She got one after giving a demo tape to a club deejay and rolled on to a string of chirpy Top Ten hits, fueled by the then-nascent music channel MTV. She wanted to act, so she landed a nervy, charismatic part in *Desperately Seeking Susan* and floated above the poorly received films that followed, holding her own on Broadway in David Mamet's *Speed the Plow*. Professionally she's had all she could desire; privately, not always. Her marriage to actor Sean Penn ended in four years, and long after, she spoke about him as her true love.

To understand the daughter, look too at the mother. Madonna lost hers to breast cancer when she was only 5. "Not having a mother, while I suffered a great deal from it, also freed me in a lot of ways," she has said. "It freed me as far as thinking what my possibilities would be." Despite her musical or thespian shortcomings, she constructed a series of provocative personas: Boy Toy, Material Girl, dominatrix, chanteuse, always the hardworking, sexy, smart girl who loved controversy almost as much as fame itself. She won her best and best-reviewed movie role in *Evita* by launching a campaign on director Alan Parker that recalled the ambition of Eva Péron herself. Names like Streep and Streisand had been kicked around, but, like everything else in her career, what Lola (once her nickname, now her daughter's) wants, Lola gets. ∎

TIME called her rise "as forceful and well-organized as D-Day." (Above: launching first world tour.)

On ending her marriage to Sean Penn: "I felt like a total failure, as any good Catholic girl would."

1990

Evita costar Antonio Banderas noted that, for both Madonna (at the premiere) and title character Eva Péron, fame "was sometimes a monster they could not control."

1996

1998

Her relationship with Lourdes's father, Carlos Leon, has ended, but Madonna says the baby still sees her dad often.

1991

Madonna sang an Oscar-nominated song from *Dick Tracy* at the Oscars but has yet to get a nod for her acting. The closest she has come is a Golden Globe for her title role in *Evita*.

1965

The first mention of divorce from Sinatra came when his lawyer presented her with the papers to sign on the *Rosemary's Baby* set.

1970

Pregnant with twins by peripatetic conductor André Previn, Farrow married him, but the pair spent only 15 days together their first year.

1988

The memoir written by Farrow (with their son Satchel, now renamed Seamus, and Dylan, renamed Eliza) chronicled Allen's hypochondria and other phobias.

Mia Farrow

For an earth mother whose nature is nurture, she found the wrong guys

SHE HAS BEEN AN ACCOMPLISHED ACTRESS, WIFE and lover of famous men and mother of 14 (10 adopted), but no matter the role or responsibility, Mia Farrow always comes off as a doe-eyed waif. The oldest daughter of seven children, she grew up Hollywood royalty—Maureen O'Sullivan was Jane in the Tarzan films, John Farrow a charismatic director. Yet the early deaths of her older brother and of her dad (in drink and decline) and a childhood bout with polio taught her "the precariousness of our place in the world." Forced into work as a shy teen, she got caught in the media spotlight playing prim Allison Mackenzie on the prime-time soap *Peyton Place* and then, at 21, marrying her first boyfriend. He was Frank Sinatra and 50. The prototypical flower child was hardly a model Rat Pack consort, and the union quickly foundered in the generation gap. (Asked by someone if he had any grass, the singer snarled he had plenty—"on my lawn.")

In 1968, Farrow's luminous portrayal of the Satan-impregnated young wife in *Rosemary's Baby* brought her stardom in her own right, but her refusal to abandon the film mid-shoot to costar in a Sinatra production had already ended the marriage. After seeking solace in India (unfortunately, just as the Maharishi whispered her mantra, she sneezed) and an eight-year marriage to maestro André Previn, Farrow was introduced in 1979 to Woody Allen. The nurturer and the neurotic became Manhattan's favorite odd couple, waving to each other through binoculars from their apartments on opposite sides of Central Park. Thirteen movies and one biological son later, a shocked Farrow discovered nude Polaroids of adopted daughter Soon-Yi on Allen's mantel, leading to a bitter public breakup and custody battle. (The judge ruled in her favor.) "The fragility is a disguise," friend Stephen Sondheim says, a sentiment Farrow, now 53, echoed by prefacing her acclaimed 1997 memoir *What Falls Away* with a poem by Theodore Roethke: "I learn by going where I have to go." ∎

1998

Farrow (with her younger children) adopted two baby girls from Vietnam during the war and a Korean girl, Soon-Yi.

1967

Neighbor Charles Boyer told her at 10, "Your life will be a wonderful one but difficult, I think." Did he know that her mother would leave her father over Ava Gardner, an ex of Mia's first husband?

Clare Boothe Luce

'Glamour girl,' playwright, politican, diplomat, wife

SHE SWITCHED CAREERS AS EASILY AS THE SCHEMING HIGH-SOCIETY ladies in her classic satire *The Women* changed hats. Dubbed by *Scribner*'s magazine the "glamour girl of publishing" in the '30s, when she worked at *Vogue*, and then as managing editor at *Vanity Fair*, she soon took her acerbic bons mots to Broadway. *Abide with Me*, a play about a drunken, sadistic husband, was a turkey as disastrous as her first marriage to an alcoholic millionaire who beat her at night and woke her by playing Yale Glee Club songs on his banjo. But her play *The Women* more than made up for it, earning critical acclaim and lifetime royalties (the 1939 movie became a cult favorite) of $2 million. By then, she had married another Yale man, Time Inc. founder Henry Luce, who launched her idea for a picture weekly, LIFE. She reported on prewar Europe for its pages, and in 1942 was elected to Congress, where she mercilessly lambasted opponents (calling a rival "the only woman who ever conducted her menopause in public"). Later Luce served as the U.S.'s first female ambassador, to Italy. Success perhaps helped her cope with her husband's rovings (and gave her more opportunity for her own), yet it could not compensate for the loss of her only child, Ann Brokaw, who died in a car crash at 19. But Luce's mind never deserted her. A year before she died at 84, in 1987, she said of a dinner companion, former British PM Edward Heath, "I was having no success at charming him, so I slayed him with pure intellectual superiority." ∎

1945

Already in Congress, Luce briefly starred in George Bernard Shaw's *Candida* in Stamford, Connecticut. She once said she owed her love for theater to Shaw and lamented, "If only I had stayed with my real interest, which was playwriting."

"Clare has always been ardently feminine," said her social secretary Letitia Baldrige. "As a result she really puts men at their ease." (In Rome, U.S. Ambassador Luce dazzled at a press club ball.)

1955

1952

Before they wed, Time Inc. kingpin Henry Luce called Boothe "the great love of my life." (The two picnicked during a visit to Madrid.)

"I've seen the future," MacLaine said in 1985. "I saw a great deal of crystal and crystal fabrics. The crystal, I suspect, is there to amplify the consciousness."

1963

"I was a prostitute in another life," MacLaine once explained to a reporter. "Which is probably why I've felt so comfortable playing prostitutes in movies like *Irma La Douce* [above] and *Sweet Charity*."

1987

CLOCKWISE FROM ABOVE: ©KEN REGAN/CAMERA 5; ©1959 BOB HENRIQUES/MAGNUM; ©GJON MILI/LIFE

1959

Fascinated by global politics, MacLaine met Soviet premier Nikita Khrushchev in L.A. Later, in 1962, she financed, and led, the first delegation of American women to China.

Shirley MacLaine

She has enjoyed numerous lives onscreen (even more off)

WHETHER ONE SUBSCRIBES, AS SHIRLEY MACLAINE DOES, TO THE NOTION that each of us has shuffled off many a mortal coil, her several incarnations within the life she's currently living (Broadway and cabaret star, film actress, author, politico, New Age avatar) are impressive enough.

Born (most recently) in 1934 in Richmond, Virginia, to a school-principal father and an artist mother, MacLaine went to New York City as a teenager armed only with encouragement and years of ballet training. She landed an understudy's job in *The Pajama Game* and got a break on the one night she was called to step in. A film producer saw MacLaine and cast her in 1955 in Alfred Hitchcock's *The Trouble with Harry*. (About that time, her brother Warren Beatty was also starting out.) Over the next decade, MacLaine would move to starring roles in *The Apartment* and *Irma La Douce* and receive three Oscar nominations. Frank Sinatra's '60s Rat Pack accepted her as its only female member. In 1970 she wrote the first of seven volumes of memoirs and took a hiatus from acting to volunteer for George McGovern's presidential campaign. Beatty wondered if his sister didn't want to enter politics herself. But MacLaine returned to screen and stage and, in 1983, won an Oscar, for *Terms of Endearment*. Yet even as critics praised her work, they joked about her belief in reincarnation. MacLaine just winked back. In an interview she said her daughter Sachi, with former husband Steve Parker, was actually the return of her own mother. And on *Tonight* in 1994, when Jay Leno congratulated her for her 60 years on this planet, she responded, "Don't you mean 4,000?" ■

NINE LIVES · **145**

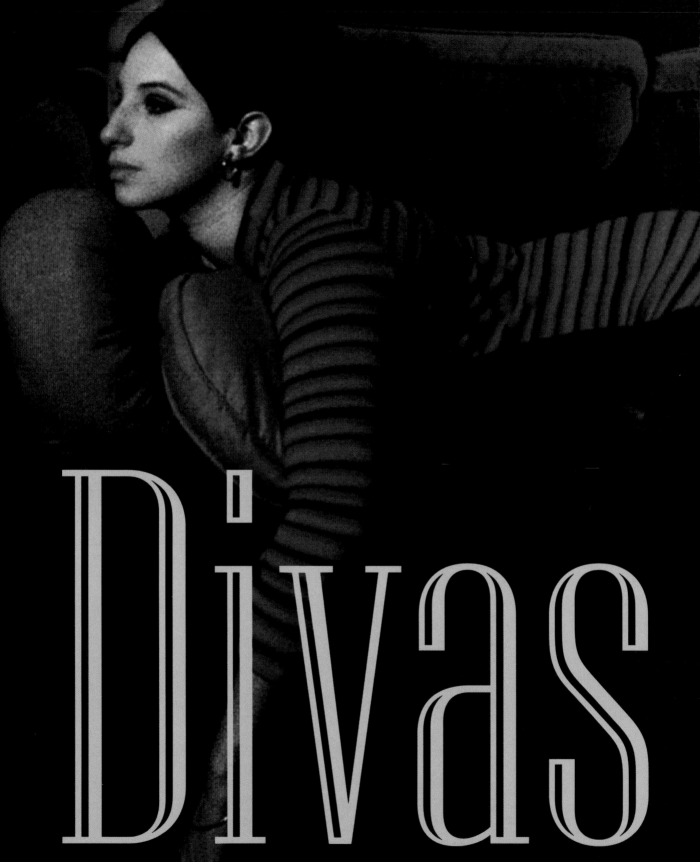

Divas

PERFORMING ARIAS OR ROYAL DUTIES, THEY'RE JUST LIKE US, ONLY MORE SO

That Voice! That Face! That unbelievably hyphenated résumé!

Barbra Streisand

Streisand (in
1967 and, inset,
shooting *Prince
of Tides in 1991*)
became the first
person to direct,
produce, cowrite,
star and sing in a
major film, *Yentl*,
in 1983.

O THIS DAY SHE NEVER SINGS AROUND THE HOUSE. Not even in the shower. During her breakthrough '60s Broadway run in *Funny Girl*, she told a reporter, "I can never understand why people laugh or cry when I sing. So the only happiness I know is real is the happiness I get from eating coffee ice cream." To be sure, Barbra Streisand realized that it was the Voice that would open the door, beginning with her 1960 debut in a Greenwich Village club. But it was the fierce drive of a fatherless girl from Brooklyn that blew the door off its hinges; she wound up collecting more gold albums than any other woman in history. At 56, she has 38. Indeed, Streisand's career is a bridge across generations. How many other singers have dueted with Louis Armstrong, Judy Garland, Neil Diamond and Celine Dion? But her real goal was to be in total charge: She started directing offbeat projects like *Yentl*; then romances with psychoanalytic overtones like *The Prince of Tides* and *The Mirror Has Two Faces*, the former costarring her son Jason, from an eight-year marriage in the 1960s to actor Elliot Gould. Her current involvement is with actor James Brolin—and backstage politics with the First Family. The year before her death the President's mother, Virginia Kelley, sat in the front row all through the stage-wary singer's 1994 tour. Fans were awed as they had been before her 28-year concert absence, back when the young Streisand summed up her success this way: "I hadda be great. I couldn't be medium. My mouth was too big." ∎

"She swooped into the air like a bird and floated down," one partner said of her signature *Dying Swan* (here in the 1920s). "At times she seemed to defy the laws of gravitation."

As ballet's exquisite swan, she fluttered off into immortality

Anna Pavlova

IN A REAL CHRISTMAS SPLURGE FOR A RUSSIAN PEASANT GIRL, HER LAUNDRESS MOTHER took Anna Pavlova to see *The Sleeping Beauty* at St. Petersburg's famed Mariinsky Theatre in 1889. Enraptured, the 8-year-old vowed to dance there herself one day, and within two years she entered the Imperial School of Ballet. It was at the time a rigid seminary where girls were not allowed to even speak to the boys who would later partner them, or, as Pavlova described it, "a convent where frivolity is banned and where merciless discipline reigns." By graduation, critics were already overcome by her ethereal beauty and haunting movements. She was, sighed one, "slender and graceful, vibrating like a reed." Pavlova achieved her goal of joining the Mariinsky troupe at 18, toured Europe (partnering the legendary Nijinsky in Sergei Diaghilev's Ballets Russes in Paris) and then traveled the globe with her own company, logging more than 400,000 miles in the prejet era. A tireless trouper, she performed her acclaimed *The Dying Swan* 4,000 times, as far away as Saginaw, Michigan, and even in a bullring in Mexico. In rare breaks, at her London home, Pavlova enjoyed cuddling her bulldogs and a pet swan she called Jack. A strict taskmaster, she practiced four hours a day, made her ballerinas dance *en pointe* until their toes bled and would drum them out of her corps if they married. Wedlock seemed not an option for Pavlova, a legacy perhaps of her monastic schooling. Despite her many lovers (including a disastrous relationship with manager Victor Dandre, who plundered her company's profits), she appeared unable to share with men the passion she expressed so movingly on the stage. On her way to perform at The Hague in 1931, she caught pneumonia. Queen Wilhelmina sent her personal physician, but Dandre, returning from a brothel, ordered her to dance that night. She couldn't, and soon after died alone in her hotel room, at 49, gazing lovingly at her swan costume. ■

For the First Lady of the American Theater, the show went on and on

Ethel Barrymore

DRAMA WAS IN THE AIR SHE BREATHED: HER GRANDMOTHER RAN A PHILADELPHIA THEATER, AND her actor father stole the name Barrymore from a poster for a show. But by 1893, when daughter Ethel turned 14, the houselights had dimmed. Her mother—also a performer—had died, and the Barrymores were scrambling for money. Ethel gave up her dream of becoming a concert pianist for a surer future in the family business. And by the time the new century dawned, the lissome actress had charmed London and was being wooed, unsuccessfully, by Winston Churchill. (She later settled for a 14-year, loveless society marriage that yielded three children.) The Barrymores—Ethel and brothers Lionel and John—conquered the stage on both sides of the Atlantic and then headed for Hollywood. They appeared together once, in the flavorful 1932 film *Rasputin and The Empress*, and Ethel won a supporting Oscar in 1944 for *None but the Lonely Heart* with Cary Grant. She did suffer from the family weakness for alcohol (she once collapsed in Denver and was booed off a London stage before finally swearing off the sauce). Although dubbed "more regal than royalty"—she once derided a houseful of Philadelphia matrons as "a moronic audience"—Barrymore happily joined fans trooping out to Ebbets Field to root for the Brooklyn Dodgers. And rivaling predecessor Sarah Bernhardt with her incessant farewell tours, she worked almost until her death, at 79. Drew's great aunt even did TV, though the grande dame of theater described it as "hell." ■

Acting teacher Stella Adler recalls seeing Barrymore (circa 1910) at midnight in a New York train station. Returning from an out-of-town show, Ethel, then in her 60s, was wrestling with her suitcases all alone.

LEFT: ARCHIVE PHOTOS; RIGHT: CULVER PICTURES INC.

Diana Ross

ANY WOMAN WHO GETS INVOLVED with Berry Gordy—and hangs in like Diana did—must be made of steel," marveled Motown labelmate Marvin Gaye. In Diana Ross's case, steel with a platinum edge. Raised in a Detroit housing project, Ross sang with her church choir, then started hanging around Motown headquarters demanding to be discovered. Gordy, the former boxer and auto worker who had founded the label, became her mentor—and her not-so-secret lover. When she wed first husband, rock promoter Robert Silberstein, Ross was pregnant with Gordy's child. Her ambition was stronger than her wispy voice, and she pushed herself to the front of an act that had once been a backup trio for other Motown groups. Under Gordy's exacting tutelage, the Supremes (later called Diana Ross and the Supremes) made a phenomenal 12 No. 1 hits, including "Where Did Our Love Go" and "Baby Love."

After leaving the group in 1970, Ross enjoyed a solo career in music and film (with such hits as *Mahogany* and *Lady Sings the Blues*, for which she earned an Oscar nomination), tarnished only by charges that she was heartless both in business and love. She stole Kiss rock star Gene Simmons away from her friend Cher, and a book by former Supreme Mary Wilson charges that Ross mistreated her and the third group member, Florence Ballard, both onstage and off, bossing them haughtily and literally pushing them out of the spotlight. These days, Ross, a 54-year-old mother of five, is remarried to Norwegian shipping magnate Arne Naess. Though close to her kids, she is frequently on tour and has no intention of retiring. Says the woman who asks her staff to refer to her as Miss Ross: "They'll have to drag me off the stage." ∎

Proud of her roots and forebears, like Marian Anderson, Price (as Aida in 1985) described herself as "a strange mixture of caviar and collard greens."

Leontyne Price

HER 1961 DEBUT AT THE METRO-politan Opera, in *Il Trovatore*, left the audience delirious for 42 minutes in perhaps the longest ovation in the history of the hallowed hall. And when the Met moved uptown to Lincoln Center five years later, the lead role opening night went to Leontyne Price. After years of resistance to black artists in the opera world, her breakthrough surprised about everybody except neighbors who had heard Price sing in her Laurel, Mississippi, church choir. Her parents, a sawmill worker and a midwife, scraped together tuition for Ohio's Central State College. That led to a scholarship to Juilliard, where composer Virgil Thomson spotted the neophyte and cast her in his 1952 revival of *Four Saints in Three Acts*. Price then toured the world in *Porgy and Bess*, marrying her costar William C. Warfield. The marriage died, but her opera career finally began to flourish, until she stepped down in 1985 to preserve her voice. "You have to guard it," she said, "so you don't lose the bloom." But Price continued giving recitals, and after one, a Boston critic raved that her "miraculous upper octave remains virtually untouched by the passage of time." That was in 1996. She was 69. ∎

"I don't always want to make the decisions," says Ross (in 1984). "But somebody has to be leader of the pack."

Glenn Close

SHE'S NOT A DIVA, SHE JUST PLAYS ONE ON STAGE AND SCREEN. There's the puppy-skinning diva in *101 Dalmations*, the bunny-stewing diva-done-wrong in *Fatal Attraction*, the aging movie diva in Broadway's *Sunset Boulevard*, the manipulative, corseted diva in *Dangerous Liaisons* and, not to forget, the comatose diva in *Reversal of Fortune*. Descended from 12 generations of Connecticut Yankees (her ancestors helped found Greenwich), Close once sang with the super-positive musical group Up With People. "Ancient history," she recently called that period in her life. Medieval history might include her earlier roles, in which she was the good girl in *The Natural* or *The Big Chill*. Then came *Fatal Attraction*, where, wielding a kitchen knife, she cut through typecasting by adding a memorable wacko to her repertoire. With the makeup off, Close, 51, now engaged to Steve Beers, a production carpenter she met while appearing in *Sunset Boulevard*, is giving her 10-year-old daughter the same kind of bucolic childhood that she had growing up on her grandparents' 500-acre estate. The only difference is that Annie also spends time on Close's film and stage sets and once lodged a complaint about Mom's role as Cruella DeVille. The key to Close's divadom is simple. She can take a cartoonish part like Cruella, eyes rolling back into a ghost-white head, because she also takes subtler parts, such as the caretaker mom in last year's *In the Gloaming*, directed by Christopher Reeve. With five Oscar nominations, three Tony Awards and one Emmy, the celebrated actress is that most rare and delightful breed of diva: the kind who knows when to give it a rest. ∎

TIMOTHY WHITE/OUTLINE

"Glennie approaches a part by jumping out the window," says pal Mary Beth Hurt of Close (at play in 1996). "And having it take shape."

Explaining why she wanted cameras allowed in Westminster Abbey to televise her 1953 coronation, Elizabeth said, "I have to be seen to be believed."

Around the palace, she is known simply as The Boss

Queen Elizabeth II

AT THE AGE OF 11, PRINCESS ELIZABETH WAS ALREADY MAKING PLANS for her future reign. "If ever I am Queen," promised Lilibet, as she was called, "the first thing I shall do will be to make a law forbidding people to ride or drive on Sunday. Horses must have a holiday!" As for herself, she rarely takes one. At 21, with her coronation still six years off, Elizabeth vowed in a public address that "my whole life, whether it be long or short, shall be devoted to your service and the service of our great Imperial Commonwealth." Although as a constitutional monarch she reigns rather than rules, the "Sov," short for sovereign, takes the job seriously. "She has probably amassed more inside knowledge of world events than any of her prime ministers," estimates one biographer. And none has been cooler under pressure. This is the Queen who continued to ride in open cars after her husband's favorite uncle, Lord Mountbatten, was assassinated by an IRA bomb in 1979. And the one who, in 1982, shrewdly kept a disturbed intruder talking on the edge of her bed until security arrived.

Duty costs. "I came to the throne when I was very young, and I never had the opportunity to bring up my children," she once told a friend. "It is something I have regretted all my life." Still, she remains a stickler for protocol: Relatives should curtsy to her before imparting a hug or kiss in public. Her dowdy image is carefully crafted to not offend her subjects, but don't underestimate her. When, early in her marriage to Prince Philip, it was rumored he was having affairs, she put him to work managing their properties and overseeing their children's educations. As the couple celebrated their 50th wedding anniversary, Philip toasted his wife, saying, "The Queen has the quality of tolerance in abundance." Only rarely, as when she misjudged public sentiment upon the 1997 death of Princess Diana, has she made a misstep—and she adjusted quickly, addressing the nation and rallying her family to stand shoulder-to-shoulder outside Buckingham Palace as the cortège passed by. Elizabeth's grandmother Queen Mary once said defensively of the royal role, "We're not supposed to be human." In QE II, Majesty meets Missus. ■

"She minds about people," said one fan of the Queen (in 1981). **"That is why she is great."**

Since '86, age has dictated carriage over horseback (top) for Trooping the Color.

After 30 years, the Queen of Soul still gets respect

Aretha Franklin

ROM THE TIME HER GOSPEL-SINGER MOTHER FORSOOK THE FAMILY, WHEN THE CHILD WAS 6, Aretha Franklin turned her pain into music. Raised by her father, Clarence—a popular Baptist minister in Detroit known as the Man with the Million-Dollar Voice—she cut her musical teeth on his traveling gospel show and picked up pointers from houseguests like Mahalia Jackson, Sam Cooke and B.B. King. At 18, the singer (already the mother of two of her four sons) took the Reverend's unexpected advice to try the pop scene in New York City. Columbia Records' legendary John Hammond—he first recorded Billie Holiday—signed her but later admitted, "Columbia was a white company that misunderstood her genius." In 1967, at the more hip Atlantic Records, she cut her breakthrough album, *I Never Loved a Man (the Way I Love You)*. The classic singles that followed—"Chain of Fools," "Think" and "(You Make Me Feel Like) A Natural Woman"—fired up the love generation, while the heart-stopping "Respect" began as an anthem for the Black Power movement and ended up as a feminist fight song. Franklin's own two marriages failed, and she continued to tour though spooked by a small-plane incident and devastated by the death of her father five years after he was shot during a botched 1979 robbery. Still truckin' at the 1998 Grammys (she has won 15), the trouper belted out "Nessun dorma" (an aria from *Turandot*) for an ailing Luciano Pavarotti, so delighting the tenor, he invited her to Italy, coaxing, "You are scared of the plane? I come to pick you up." If there were any doubts of her pop supremacy, they were resolved a month later at a Manhattan concert called *Divas Live*. The soaring voice and sassy stage presence of Aretha, 56, reduced her billed costars—Mariah Carey, Gloria Estefan and Celine Dion—to virtual, and willing, backup singers. ■

She remade her campy self safe (almost) for Disney

Bette Midler

"M Y THING IS ALL SEND-UP," BETTE MIDLER CONFIDES, AND NOT without pride. In order to live her girlhood dream of belting out bygone goldies on club stages in a time when the past was passé, Midler sang tongue-in-cheek. But how else to make "Boogie Woogie Bugle Boy" a hit in the 1970s? Raised in the only Jewish family in a Samoan neighborhood in Honolulu, young Bette, the namesake of one of her mother's fave actresses, made her move first to Hollywood (ironically, in a bit part in James Michener's *Hawaii*). Next came New York City, where she honed her trash-as-art sensibility performing in a gay bathhouse with pianist Barry Manilow. These now notorious shows became the basis for her *Divine Madness* revue on Broadway. But besides camp, she could also vamp—for sentiment—and did in *The Rose*, a 1979 film loosely based on the life of Janis Joplin. In 1986 she developed a new persona: the kooky, rich housewife in Disney's *Down and Out in Beverly Hills*. Then round about the time she and her businessman-turned-performance-artist husband Martin von Haselberg became parents of a daughter came her tearjerker *Beaches*. Its equally soapy theme song, "The Wind Beneath My Wings," won her fourth Grammy. Now, at 52, Midler can look back over a blessedly varied oeuvre and pick which Bette she wants to be: the goddess of concert camp, warbling showstoppers in a mermaid getup? The star of custom comedies like *The First Wives Club*? Or the drama queen of torch songs and modern-day weepies? Fortunately, the Divine Miss M (as she deified herself) needn't choose only one. ∎

"I just go where the light is glittering," said Midler (in 1996). "and pretty much do what would enchant me."

Over-the-top was too low by half for this drama queen

Bette Davis

SHE HAD BETTE DAVIS EYES BEFORE THEY WERE FASHIONABLE. With a ruddy and unsymmetrically angular face, Davis didn't even approximate Hollywood's beauty standard. No matter: She lowered her weighty eyelids, set her sight on stardom and fought for it successfully. On Broadway, in Ibsen's *The Wild Duck* at age 21, she moved one director to say, "My God! She's made of lightning!" That part led to screen tests and movie contracts and began a career that would garner 10 Oscar nominations and shatter the mold for film stars. LIFE called her breakthrough part, in 1934's *Of Human Bondage*, "probably the best performance ever recorded on screen by a U.S. actress." Davis was unusual, not only for her looks, which audiences eventually warmed to, but for the fact that she chose her own scripts. She was a shrewd judge of film writing and characterization—and of dialogue. She often edited lines out but knew not to mess with whoppers like "Fasten your seat belts, it's going to be a bumpy night" *(All About Eve)* or "What a dump!" from *Beyond the Forest*.

Growing up in Lowell, Massachusetts, young Ruth Elizabeth Davis knew she had to act from grade school. Her father, who had never wanted children, was withholding, but her mother was affectionate and encouraging. The combination no doubt fueled her ambition but undermined her own relationships later in life.

"I guess I'm larger than life," mused Davis (at home in Los Angeles in 1939, browsing through the morning papers). "That's my problem."

The one man who matched her power and treated her respectfully was William Wyler, Davis's director in *Jezebel*. "I adored him," she said of the love she never married because, astonishingly, she had neglected to read the hand-delivered note that contained his proposal. Thinking Davis was ignoring his offer, Wyler married another woman. From her own four marriages, darkened by competition, infidelity and spousal abuse, she came away with this wisdom: "[Marriage] takes three things—communication, separate bedrooms and separate baths." Deciding she was "a failure as a wife," she rededicated herself to work and continued acting in film and TV until two years before her death, at 81, from cancer, in 1989. She lived to become the first woman given the American Film Institute's Life Achievement Award, and to be the basis for a 1977 pop song. Singer Kim Carnes gave her gold record for "Bette Davis Eyes" to the actress, and a pleased Davis hung it in her living room. "My grandson," said Davis, "has gained a whole new respect for me." ∎

"She was difficult to work with," said Ann Sothern of Davis (in 1989). "God bless you, Bette, and mellow out. Don't be ordering everybody around in heaven."

LEFT: ALFRED EISENSTAEDT/LIFE; RIGHT: FABIEN ESTIVALS/SYGMA

Index